Born and raised in the suburbs of Chester, Rik Waddon found a passion for sports, which in turn gifted him the escape from the stigma of having a disability that followed him around as a young child. Now over three decades on from a road traffic accident at just five years of age that saw him knocked off a bike, he revels in his achievements of being a World Champion and Double Paralympic Cycling medalist. Rik has no plans on retirement just yet as he has unfinished business at the Paralympic Games with sights set on Tokyo's 2020 Games.

I dedicate this book to Grace, a person of courageous spirit and single-minded determination.

Rik Waddon

A Saving Grace

AUSTIN MACAULEY PUBLISHERS™

LONDON • CAMBRIDGE • NEW YORK • SHARJAH

A CIP catalogue record for this title is available from the British Library.

ISBN 9781528989411 (Paperback)
ISBN 9781528989428 (Hardback)
ISBN 9781528989435 (ePub e-book)

www.austinmacauley.com

First Published (2021)
Austin Macauley Publishers Ltd
25 Canada Square
Canary Wharf
London
E14 5LQ

There are so many people in my life's journey that have been there along the way through the tough times and the good times. You may occasionally think that you are treading the lonely path yourself, but always in the background, there are people going the extra distance to help and encourage you along. There are a fair few people right from the onset of this book that I want to acknowledge, a lot of the names will mean absolutely nothing to the general public but mean an incredible amount to me. The biggest gratitude I hand to my family. Everyone leads busy lives, but they have been there through everything, and from year 5 of my life when things altered somewhat to these last few months, my mother has been the rock to keep my feet planted and stop me from doing anything stupid, 3- and 4-hour convocations on the phone at obscure hours of the day she was there to just listen even when I was at the lowest of points and tipping myself off the edge. To my dad for everything that he taught me as a youngster, all the times he picked me up and for the journey. My brother Ryan, sister-in-law Nikki, and my niece and nephew Florence and Alfie, who bring a smile to my face each time that I see them. My aunt Julie that would drop everything if I needed an escape. Thank you for being there, it means the world to me even though I may never say it or make much reference to my feelings.

My good lifetime friend, James, we may only see each other once every few years, but the good times we had as youngsters will keep that bond strong.

Michael Jones, not just a father-in-law but also someone I was able to rely on under any circumstances, thanks for being there when it counted!

This leads me on to those from the start of my sporting career: Peter McNulty, my former high school head teacher, who ignited my cycling juices after his showing of the 1989 Tour de France stage in one of our very disorganised maths lessons. Geoff Chaplin, Gerry Robinson and Graham Ashbrook of the Chester Road Club really did show me the very basics of getting started when it came to riding and racing a bike; they nurtured me through my early days as a junior rider and installed the discipline that is needed to become successful. Dave Baker inspired my international career somewhat, a guy that was always there to lend a hand or borrow out equipment if I asked, a great ambassador for young riders.

I must thank all those that have supported me and backed my ambitions. Carl Jenkins at the specialised concept store in Chester along with Dave Quinn and Dave Parry that seem to go out of their way whenever I ask for help – you guys have really been there when it counted. My next special thanks goes to the unsung heroes, the people that work behind closed doors, the people that really have put me back together. Andrea Hemmingway, who worked on my broken body for many years at the English Institute of Sport in Manchester along with Phil Burt. The coaching staff that I have worked with over the years, Ken Matterson, whom I first came across in 2001 and really showed me just a completely new level to training at the start of my international career; Marshall Thomas was for 5 years really the backbone that transformed me into a track rider with his endless experience and knowledge; Dave Mellor for simply his man-management skills that he was able to share with me and keep my feet planted firmly; Chris Furber, a massive influence on my career who coached me through two Paralympic Games, countless world championships and dealt with my unpredictability and toys out of the pram situations when they would pop up which was quite a lot. There is the backroom staff at British Cycling that worked tirelessly on things that I would know nothing about. Alison Johnson to name but one, my very first point of contact back in July 2000, the faceless woman that I would communicate with for almost a year before I actually had the privilege to meet her; all the mechanics that seem never to be without a spanner in their hands regardless of the time of day and the kit room guys that I would only see locked away in their windowless grotto of anything and everything to do with bikes.

In my later years, Richy Bott of the University of Chester and the time he gave to transform me from the track sprinter of the 2012 games into a medal-winning World Cup endurance rider of 2016 – you guys really are the building blocks of hundreds of athletes that you not only physically coach but also mentor.

Other acknowledgements I feel strongly about are those whose lives and paths that I have crossed through my career: teammate Barney Storey whom I roomed with on my first Great Britain debut event back in 2001; Darren Kenny, my career long Great Britain teammate in which we have shared some pretty awesome untold times around the world along with some fantastic racing and head-to-head battles of our own; Jody Cundy, again a great roommate to have had during my career, a bit of a tech boffin and all round gadget man, also the head guy of my domestic team over the past 6 or 7 years which I can't thank him enough for all the support that he and the para-cycling team gave to me throughout that time.

My next set of acknowledgements really are more personal to the individuals, as they have been life-changing in one way or another over the past 12 months, and I felt that to acknowledge them as a collective wouldn't sit with my ethics.

Cai, you showed, over the 8 months that I had the privilege to work with you, your maturity excelled and I felt very humbled to be a part of that period of your life. Miles, from first meeting you to our last day working together, it really had been a developing journey, to witness you unfold and shine in the way that you did does give me a great satisfaction to be part of that path with you. Rhiannon, don't run away from something that could be amazing, life is full of outstanding unknowns, working with you was a scream, there were times when I told you that I couldn't do it anymore as that was because I struggled to keep a straight face as you were so funny, especially with the Bunsen burner and charcoal, there was only so many times that I could bite my tongue through trying to stay professional in my work. Ella, your path is what you make it, there is no set route, everything that you do makes an imprint, make those imprints be part of your success. Liam, don't let others dictate your future, I wish I could have spent more time working with you, you have the ability to be as good as you want to be, your sporting passion to win is second to none, harness that passion and channel it. Molly, I could write a chapter on you alone, your personal fight with life is extraordinary, always keep getting up, never let it win, you have too much to offer life. Grace, your determination and courage will be the fuel to your success, working with you not only impacted positively on your life and showed you that anything is possible, but it also changed my life, work extra hard at everything that you set your mind to, follow your rugby passion, it will be the making of you, you have a determination that I have rarely seen in anybody before, use it to your advantage.

Thank you to everyone else that has been part of my life, you know who you are and without you, I wouldn't really have a story to tell.

Synopsis

The title for my Autobiography *A Saving Grace* came about after my inspirational mentoring work that I have carried out in schools for the past six years.

After a road traffic accident at the age of just five years old left me with a disability from a sustained head injury, I struggled on my route through school academically; never really having the coordination to play sport either, I found myself in a somewhat world with no direction. It was only in my later school years that I took up bike riding and fell in love with the sport developing a passion and drive beyond anything that I have felt before. This guided me to my Paralympic sporting career which spanned over some 10 years as a professional cyclist achieving accolades such as world and European champion, world record holder, and representing at two Paralympic Games, one of which was the London 2012 games. Performing at a high level brought with it the demands, pressures as well as politics of professional sport. Unable to show weakness or mental health problems, you just had to get on with things no matter how difficult the situation became.

After the 2012 games, I was gifted the opportunity to work within the education system with difficult-to-reach students as a mentor to assist them with their challenges. I developed a huge positive impact nationwide with the work that I was doing which on a personal level became a new-found passion. In 2018, a student that I was working with was in such a dark place that my work became an almost 24-hour-a-day job, and after asking for extra help via outside agencies nothing was put in place for this one student that I took as a total disrespect for her life.

From my own experiences of self-harming through my sporting career as an adult, I could not just sit back and watch this 14-year-old tread through similar anguish and turmoil within the school environment. I made a promise to myself that I would be there for her no matter how bad the days were… After months and an unimaginable number of hours' work spent with her, after she first disclosed that she wanted to take her own life, my work came to an end. The feeling of saving a life is something that I hope not many people will have placed before them as the pressure and responsibility that you deal yourself in the initial moments is huge!

The months that followed that period of time were catastrophic for myself, my own mental health took an unexpected turn, inconsolable from the fall out that I was dealt, I found myself in a suicidal situation after an allegation was made against me by a third party.

Unable to deal with the frustrations of authorities, as well as them misconstruing the facts, and being unable to comprehend the situation that surrounded the intricate work that I did with the student to turn her life around and keep her alive left me at a point of no return.

In the midst of misery under my own dark emotional tent, I was able to cling onto my own life using the strength shown by the 14 year-old-student that had herself at a desperate time of reaching out.

Foreword

I first met Rik Waddon a few days before the start of the London Paralympics in 2012. I was working for Channel Four, and Rik was about to win a silver medal on the track. Accompanied by a camera crew and without the authorisation of his team press office, Rik invited me into the athlete's village for a guided tour of his accommodation. Just as we were filming, we got busted. I was ejected, and Rik had his wrist slapped. Not that he appeared to give a damn.

This was typical Rik Waddon. He's a man who's never conformed particularly comfortably to that which the world expects of him. He does what he wants to, and he does it with great style.

Rik's battles on various fronts have been considerable. What follows on these pages is an unflinching look at the hard times he's endured, and how he has come through it, still with his sense of fun and humanity intact. I urge you to read it, and to ask yourself, 'if this was me, how would I have coped.'

I salute him.

Ned Boulting

Introduction

November 4th 2018, it's 1.54 am, the sound of the wind howling across the roof tiles and through the branches in the lonely standing tree across the road, the flickering light from an over-enthusiastic security light beams through the not-so-quite closed curtains that I drew together just a few hours earlier. 'I'm at probably the lowest point in my life right now', in the last week I have self-harmed due to the stresses of the past month or so. Obviously to put into words how I feel right at this moment in time is beyond me, I think one simple word, or phrase to start with, would be 'tired'…

In some ways right now, my life seems to be a million miles from where it was just a few years ago as a Paralympic athlete and a professional cyclist riding on the Great Britain cycling team. With mental health issues resurfacing and carrying the same traits, but with a more savage impact mounting as a result of having to deal with the frustrations of working within the education system, I have never been in such an overwhelming dark emotional tent as I am right at this moment in time. I look across at my medication and wonder to myself: just how easy would it be to take the lot at once, with my logic-thinking processes being clouded by misery, as I move from my bed, shuffling my feet towards the door, my thoughts turn to writing. From what has happened in the last week I have taken inspiration to write this book, to express my feelings as to the one specific thing that has turned things around in my life, the saviour to my being. Life is about platforms, moving from one level to another, they may be long periods of time, or just brief encounters, but it's about what we can take from these moments that will lead us into the next.

Chapter 1
What's the Point!

I once heard the saying "Even Einstein started at zero" and from my understanding of that statement, it says that anyone can achieve anything that they set out to do, but when you are faced with difficult situations time and time again within your own life, the moment of impact can be so devastating that even the brightest of stars would have trouble reflecting its light. When somebody is sitting on the opposite side of a desk from you, looks directly at you, and just wipes across your life, and takes everything that you have worked for, and doesn't even blink, tells you that you're not up to your job, and that they believe that you should possibly think about another career path. "Oh, so this is the point where my life is going to end."

How do I even start to process this? As I sat there watching the mouth of this person still speaking, but unable to hear what else was being directed at me, I knew the darkest and most unbearable sad chapter in my life was here with the awkward questions and terrifying fear of embarrassment, but I sense "déjà vu" here sat in the same position pre the 2012 Paralympic Games rider review with the GB Team in 2011. Suddenly all I thought of was the aftermath of that occasion, the depression, turmoil, and self-abuse that followed. Was this to be yet the same path that I was to fall ill of, even with all my skills that I had learnt from performing under pressure, and keeping my cool at some of the huge sporting events on the world stage, I knew that none of the coping skills were going to help me in this situation.

I struggled as a child growing up and going through school with a disability, my anxiety would crush me every time, it would fester and grow like an uncontrollable bacteria, it would control and hold my life. Mental health issues had limited my ability to shine and develop as a child, leaving me to be scared of my own shadow, even though at the time I knew nothing of mental health and the effects that it was having on me. Ten years ago I had suffered from panic attacks that were brought on by concerns over a health issue that I had at the time, and they ruled over my everyday life for a long time back then, would they also be relighted as a consequence of the current situation. I knew I had to switch back on and listen to what else this person was saying, but I didn't know what to say or do, every thought was shrouded in absolute fear.

All I could think about was that it has taken me two and a half years to rebuild my life after the collapse of my marriage which in itself is something that you never really get over, you just tend to deal with it, putting those anxious thoughts to the deepest parts of your mind hoping that they will never return, and then also dealing with what may have looked like at the time as the end of my sporting career when my funding stream ended which was to say the least 'my life', and now facing another ending that is a passion that I found that was that of the same magnitude. The intense feeling of achievement that I got each time I sat on the start line of any major world competition, how was I to go on from here. OK, so yeah it would be unwise to not question my life as all my beliefs and dreams had been put into this.

Suspended from my new job and career path, told to cease doing my voluntary work and have no contact with a family that I was very fond of were the orders that I was issued.

The worthlessness in the hours, days, weeks and months that followed that meeting were a mirror image of my contract termination from the GB team, two very different passions in my life now being executed in the same way. It's easy to behave as if nothing is wrong, even when you have good mental health. I felt stagnant, aware that I had to endure these painful emotions, but also worried that I may never truly feel better. Life just continues around you no matter how much your own world has been shattered. As soon as I left that meeting and ventured back to my car, normalities would heave into view but I did not want it. A car horn would catch me as I stumbled onto the road without a care, a cyclist shouted out as I stepped in front of him almost colliding with him, again not really taking in the world in motion. I suspected that in a few weeks all would be over with this awful mix up, but still be locked in my narrow space, anxiety and depression as my only companions, not knowing that the fallout would in fact be more catastrophic than was first even imaginable, with not just myself feeling the effects.

My armour had taken a battering and was broken, the solid exterior that would normally hold me in good stead, exposed to everyone. Immediately, I felt everybody was looking at me, I felt them talking, a thousand eyes looking down on me making their judgement, I could not run nor hide, but just try and find my route through the valley of uncertainty as I navigated the solace journey back to my car. Without a thought I had covered several streets in the opposite direction to where I had left the car hours earlier, nothing was making sense, I had nowhere to turn, each direction I looked in was just an empty void, but somehow shrouded in moments of desperation and utter confusion, my anxiety hitting like with no warning, I had to find order. Suddenly thoughts of my competition days arrived in my vision recalling coping mechanisms that were drilled into me, 'fight, flight, fear' the chimp management that was developed by Dr Steve Peters, a ground-breaking model that's helped athletes to perform under pressure, but none of this was making sense. All those events where I could flick a switch and just focus on delivery of what I had trained for was now like an unstoppable lottery machine, I turned but was unable to find a route of logical thinking. Somehow amidst the whirlwind of emotions I found my way back to my car and on to home. Anger, frustration and trepidation haunted me for several weeks following this day. The fear of starting from zero at the age of 41 was not something I wanted to think about, but the reality started to creep in, knocking on the door with no warning and as it doesn't just work 9 'til 5 Monday to Friday it quite often calls in the middle of the night waking me from the broken sleep that I grab whenever I can. Without a job and friends at a limited existence, filling my time was to be the most difficult, going from window to window on a daily basis and with my phone in my hand as my only friend and gateway to the outside world. My anxieties were becoming worse, locking myself into a deeper depression, a phobia of not wanting to be around people was starting, the fear of stepping outside of the house, going to the shop was becoming a stretch to the imagination, but things were to get worse, building up the courage to go and see my doctor was one of immense anxiety, but what followed that initial visit was much worse. After leaving the doctor's surgery I returned home, grabbed my sleeping bag, turned my phone off and left the house. Five days of nothing, no people, just me, a time where I had thoughts of taking my own life because I could not see a point to anything, I had nothing to show for my life, I was ashamed and embarrassed of my life. Before I left the house, I self-harmed, not something that I am proud of, but at the time it was a release of feeling worthlessness. I had self-harmed a few weeks previous when I first started feeling this way after the first initial concern was brought to my attention, it's not something you plan nor think about in the lead up to harming yourself, it's spontaneous and leads itself. I drove and drove and ended up in Penrith in Cumbria. I had no plan, no thought. I sat in an Italian restaurant, eating some pasta. There were very few people in the restaurant, but my anxieties were telling me that they knew why I was there even though I had never set eyes on these people ever before. I made quick of the pasta and then left, I drove some more and found myself in Buttermere, nestled up in the mountains of the Lake District. It was pitch black with no light pollution, I wanted some sleep but could not settle, my mind wondering through a field of uncertainty. I made the decision to drive some more. I was hungry and thirsty and was in need of some caffeine; I found a Starbucks and sat until they closed, again my mind undecided what to do. I just drove and found myself at 1.30 in the morning tucked away at the back of a pub carpark, I must have fallen asleep as I was woken at 6.30 by the sound of rain hitting the roof, lay curled up in some discomfort on the backseat in my sleeping bag, staring at the ceiling. I was trying to make sense of the previous day, but it was almost like I had a memory block, a space in time that did or did not happen, and then a brief reminder from a snag of the cuts on my arm on the inside of my jumper that the moment was very real.

As each day passed, I was searching for a point, a focus, a small but meaningful something that would keep me breathing and serve as a lifeline. All I could think about was why I was here in this unjustified situation, the one thing that had all the emotions, the rights and the wrongs, the reason as to why my anxieties were so strong and forceful, how was I to channel them into another direction, and then it hit me on day three in the middle of the night of my spontaneous trip; 'write it all down', but from that one single thought came something greater, a book! A book of my life, my autobiography, it was something that I had wished around in my head in previous years, but never really put into action. It was also something that I hadn't ever done before, my reading and writing skills were non-existent, I had read only one book in my entire life when I was younger, my English GCSE result from school had been a grade G and I had never engaged in any sort of writing in great length since my school days. I was at zero, the only way from here was up, to make something from nothing, but I needed a plan, a structure surely, I mean that is how the professionals do it, but I wasn't a professional. My anxieties were once again creeping in, putting the doubts into my mind, battering me just how they have done over the past few days, weeks and years whenever I have had any idea of a project, beating me every time, but not this time. I was spurred on; all I could think of was the one person that was the centre of all this dismay. This person was to be my inspiration that I opted for in this misery that I was suffering. I'd never written before and I had spent the past six or seven years giving in to my negative thoughts of never being any good at anything academic, letting it calcify and build up layer upon layer until it had become too strong for me to even have the smallest of ideas of writing. Maybe the sudden urge to write was a mental manifestation of this desire to break the mould of my subconscious thinking,

I am about to turn 42 in a couple of months' time and terrified I would use the age thing as an excuse to just retreat, to be scared of my own shadow and life itself. I wasn't ready to write, say a huge amount, and I had jotted a few things down in the days prior to me going AWOL, but it was more out of frustration, but then all I could think about was this situation and the circumstances of how I have gotten to this low point and state of anguish and terror.

My whole life I have put other people first, in everything that I have done, I have always been the person to take the hit time and time again with the outcome always ending up with myself placed back at zero, so why was this to be any different. Well, it wasn't, the only way that I was to make the outcome any different was to actually channel every last bit of energy that I had no matter how difficult the days would be into writing this book with one person in mind, that one person that came to me and asked me for help, that person that was determined and would not stop asking until they got what they wanted. The determination to reach out when you are in a dark place and to keep asking time and time again takes courage, I needed to harness that, and use that person's situation to fuel me. This was to be my saviour, my lifeline to get me through and make the days' worth getting up from my bed. My anxieties would still be there, but now I had a focus, it would be easy for me to get on my bike and go out each day, to slip back into a comfort zone that I knew, but I needed something to have an impact on the misery, a meaningful purpose. Sometimes we have to do stuff that scares us, something that is so far out of character that all you think about is that it is impossible, that was to be it, the tool I opted for in the midst of despair, but how was I to do this? I felt vulnerable, very unsafe, and alone, my only refuge was sitting in my car. I would spend hours just driving around anywhere, and then when I pulled up at home I would continue to just sit there, the snugness of the chair hugged my body, the shell of the car wrapped around me like a blanket, I never wanted to leave this secure space. I needed to overcome this and stop running to my car each time I felt the insecurity of being somewhere different, but my anxieties would scream at me each time and it would become a battle in itself. I figured a strategy whereas I would drive somewhere and sit in a café to write. At first I felt slightly ashamed – as if I was doing something perverse that shouldn't be seen, I mean who was I, just someone that didn't achieve academically in my younger years so what right did I have sitting there attempting to write an autobiography, a book, something much bigger and more in depth than say-and-training diary that I had been used to just filling in with just short comments because I hated writing in any shape or form. The thought of putting pen to paper would make my stomach churn over as now I had to deal with the harrowing thoughts of typing which were a thousand times worse as I hate spending any sort of time in front of a keyboard, people would laugh I am sure, I mean I would laugh at me.

As I began to type out line after line, I realised that maybe it wasn't such a good idea, perhaps I had gone in above my head with this, after all my vocabulary isn't that advanced, my catalogue of words is quite often passed to me via television programmes that I have watched with me then quickly scribbling down anything that I have heard that sounds like a great word to drop into conversations that I may have in the future, and then researching the meaning so as I wouldn't look like a total drop out if I was to use them in the wrong term. Throughout my life if I couldn't do something well on the first attempt, I was prone to quit, it was embarrassingly clear to me that I was not writing well, or getting better at it, and yet, much to my own quiet disbelief, I carried on, for the first couple of weeks I was having to redo and go over what I had written which was turning into a really lengthy process of three steps forward and four steps backwards. Part of my brain seemed to switch off which left me in a somewhat nonchalant place of being, but this was in itself becoming frustrating as my rhythm of writing was in fits and spats, but two things were becoming clear. The first was that when I was writing I didn't feel quite so sad and worthless, my mind would quieten down; some part of my brain seemed to switch off and cede control for the time that I was writing, I wouldn't think of my situation, nor question my own being. The second thing, which was even more valuable, was that I noticed that I wasn't feeling anxious, this was gaining me some confidence once again. For years I had not wanted to read or write, but within a month I had wrote out almost 60000 words, how was this possible, had I missed something in my younger years that could have served me a better education, had my own brain denied me. I wasn't obsessed by these newfound questions about myself or the thoughts that I was having, it was miraculous to me.

My mind, accustomed to frightening me for so many years if I ever wanted to do anything different with endless 'what if' thoughts, or even happy to torment me with flashbacks of some of my worst experiences and ordeals. Anxiety has been with me for such a long time now it seems as if I have had it forever, I can't remember being any different, it's ebbed and flowed over the years. At the age of 17, I developed a nervous breathing habit, I thought nothing of it at the time and put it down to a growing up thing, whenever I had a bad thought or a negative feeling I would make a hissing sound by emptying my lungs of every bit of air until I was close to fainting. It then would happen when I was out during training on my bike and would disrupt my sessions each day, it became a habit as if to rid my body of bad feelings as quickly as possible, but that would happen each day, I recall trying to break the frequency by saying to myself. "OK, this is the last time." There was no winning though, it would just keep happening, it was as though I had to keep doing it, before I would go anywhere or enter a room I would have to perform this ritual that would actually piss me off, but I knew if I didn't do it then things would only turn out bad, this routine would take up time and paralyse my day.

It's believed that your brain does these type of things in an attempt to protect you, but it only makes you feel much worse and you are unable to get back to reality no matter how hard you try, like trying to override a safety mode on a modern day motor vehicle. This was the first real point in my life that I started to consciously recognise my anxieties, for sure I must have had many times going through school, but I just didn't think of them in the same way. Anxiety is in itself a clever thing, the moment that you've got a handle on one thing it will throw you another one and quite often much worse than the previous. It's no cure running away from a mental illness or any sort of illness for that matter. After returning to my doctor for a second time he wrote out a prescription, I sat there and once again anxiety showed itself. It's ironic, I know, you go to the doctors thinking you're going to be cured but end up coming out feeling worse – that's anxiety for you. I had also been referred for counselling so now I had the added trepidation of having to talk to a total stranger about my shit. I would look at the small box of pills, one a day and your woes will be cured "as easy as that"; that was my understanding anyway, but I was not so easily convinced, it wasn't going to cure anything, just put a temporary block on things. Is this what I really wanted, to be under a false pretence, my anxieties would still be there, just unable to show themselves, in many respects I wanted to feel these intense anxious thoughts, to pick them to bits and understand them, I didn't want to be patched up by medication nor have to talk to someone on a half hour phone call once a month, what's the point. I want to feel my emotions and be able to deal with them, this makes me a stronger person, it shapes me and has done for a huge portion of my life so far. For some people medication is the correct thing, for others it may be some other form of therapy. Your body and mind are the best instrument that you will ever own, your own ability is quite often beyond your imagination, but you just need to understand how to tap into it to unlock your potentials. I didn't take the medication nor did I even start it, I spoke to a counsellor on a handful of occasions but used it as just a random person to chat to. My main focal point was to write this book, having the mindset of a champion, a winner from my sporting days, that itself is something that you cannot teach anyone, that ability is ingrained in you, to achieve no matter what the odds in any condition, the anxieties are always going to be there, sometimes much more difficult than others. This has been by far the most trying of them all in my life, but I am dealing with things and have done something by writing this biography that I never thought I would do, they may be clever in their own way that each time they try to deliver something worse, but the anxieties this time have possibly delivered me a key to unlock a part of my inner self that has been kept at bay for many years.

Chapter 2
September '82

After returning home from school one afternoon, I grabbed my bicycle from the garden shed and waved to my mother who was standing at the back door as I left to go to my friend's house. The next thing I knew I was laying down and could hear the faint sounds of a siren, vaguely seeing the flashing of blue light as I stared up at a white ceiling drifting in and out of a sleep like feeling. At the next recollection I was in a bed sat up, I remember very little about what I thought was going on to what actually was going on, it all seemed a bit of a jumbled up mess which I was struggling to make sense of, certain aspects are quite clear, for instance those times that we all have in our lives that imprint on our memories and so-called scar us for the entirety of our lives.

For myself it was the days of tests and monitoring that I had to endure, being put into a CT scanning machine, I remember crying each time I was slowly moved into place, that dark narrow tube that even for a fully grown adult can be a daunting experience, but for myself at just five years old, if you can imagine somebody holding your head under water while trying to breathe through a straw then that's the feeling I can only relate it to.

Another harrowing feeling was each time that I was transported to and from other areas of the hospital was that I was either carried or moved around in a pushchair; this was obviously because my legs were not working which again I was unable to comprehend as I didn't fully know why I was there. My arms and hands were of the same non-functional condition which just added to my frustration of not being able to understand what had happened.

The most horrific and frightening thought that remains in my subconscious mind even today is when I could not speak any words, the only thing that I could do at the time was make little noises, but could not project them outwardly, it was almost like a sound that only I could hear, a murmur, a sound that when I think about it these days just completely haunts me, because it takes me right back to when I was laying on the road just minutes after the accident. If I shut my eyes even now so many decades after the accident and make those low murmuring sounds I can actually bring back all the feelings of those initial moments; the hurt, the helplessness of my almost lifeless body that I was losing grip of at the roadside on that September afternoon.

Those memories no matter what they relate to in anyone's life whether it be a difficult time through your childhood, losing a loved one, work related stresses or anything that has a mental energy sapping effect or shock will leave its imprint forever. For myself it not only left the mental scarring, but also a physical one which is a daily reminder that I can never steer away from nor change. To accept from such a young age that things will never be the same ever again is something that I subconsciously must have not signed the contractual paperwork.

As the days past and I lay in that hospital bed, in between being whisked off for tests and to rehabilitation, there was to the right of my bed a huge window that went the full width of the ward that I was on and threw in the light past the trees that were just outside, just below the central point of the window a toy garage sat on a wooden table, on top of this garage there had been placed a small car. The sunlight would catch on the plastic windows of the garage each morning and that would in turn catch my attention and draw my eyes to the car, obviously I could not gather anyone's attention, my mother and father would sit beside my bed, but I was unable to communicate either by movement or speech, it was an almost silent world that I found myself in with only my eyes to capture the events of each day.

From time to time I remember being taken to a small room with low lighting that gave off the same effect of that of a low energy light bulb of today's standard, it gave me a sense of calmness and a feeling of security. Before my eyes in this room there were toys for all ages, and a huge array of children's books that stood out with their bright colours and punchy cartoon character-like illustrations that drew me into a different world that was so very different to the one I was actually experiencing at that time. It was a room that I didn't want to leave once in there, a comfortable environment that removed me from my conscious chaotic thoughts and placed me amongst harmless surroundings, and feelings that I often go back to even today in order to seek tranquillity.

I had no perception of time, but when I was wheeled or carried from that room I was leaving that comfort zone not by choice, but by order that somebody else had instructed, the sinking feeling each time that happened was again a memory that will never leave my mind. Whether it was being transferred to the physiotherapy room, or to be run through more rigorous tests, the journey always passed that small room where on first approach I would feel jovial and overwhelmed with excitement, when in fact nine times out of ten, I was being taken to the CT scanning area and being placed through the traumatic feeling of laying inside a tube where my eyes would be fixed on the casing above my head that was just inches away from my face with no other perception of anything around me, being unable to move my arms or legs, I just had to lay there making those murmuring sounds, those inner screams that I could not project outwards of my body, and that I still have thoughts about today.

As days turned into nights, and then into weeks the daily routine would never change, I started to receive more visitors, and I remember certain gifts arriving at my bedside, but still I could not communicate, one gift was a small wooden handheld toy that was in the shape of an H; and about eight inches in size, it had a piece of entwined string stretched across the top at one end of the toy and positioned in the centre of the string was a trapeze artist that when you squeezed the opposite end of the 'H'-shaped toy, the trapeze figurine would spin around like a modern-day Max Whitlock for hours of fun and as you can imagine watching someone else play with it as I still had no coordination or feeling in my hands was just the medicine I had wished so hard for.

When I look back now, I think the toy itself must have been marketed for the senior citizens of that era as this toy didn't even have any colour or character to it. I also believe that I still have it tucked away in a drawer somewhere so perhaps once I retire, I will be able to put it to its full potential.

So the day finally came when I started to show signs of change in the direction that my family and doctors had been hoping for. After weeks of continued sunlight bouncing off the toy garage over by the window that would catch my attention every time without fail, and the car on its roof never having been played with, the very first word to escape from my closed-down body was "garage". I spat it out like a hot chip just from the wrapping. I don't think it was the garage I actually wanted, I think it was more the car, but obviously my brain was trying to rewire itself, and amidst the excitement and jubilation it decided to play a word association game with my parents, who I hadn't spoken to for weeks, that sat at the side of the bed. I can only imagine what feelings they must have had at that one point. I mean after weeks of listening to my murmurs, all the other thoughts, anxieties and stresses that must have overwhelmed them so much during this period, then for them to hear that first word must have been a profound feeling of an unbelievable sense of being.

It was at this point that things started to move forward at a steady rate, the neurological connections had started, my brain was slowly processing and lighting up new channels to deliver the signals that my thoughts were asking of it. Of course, this comes with its downs; mental fatigue was, and still is, a huge factor for me. Even now my concentration levels drop off after just ten minutes of focus on anything that I am doing, but again the brain is an amazing computer, in fact it's the best computer that you will ever own; it repairs your body, it automatically runs things in the day time when your mind and thoughts are on other things, it has a night mode to make sure you keep breathing in the dead of night. In fact, it does everything that you don't ask it to do, for instance you don't suddenly wake in the morning and think 'I must make sure my internal organs work today', it just happens, that's magic!

The more words I started to put together the higher the fatigue, but it was starting to open up other pathways, my hands were starting to gain some sort of function which gave me the ability to push the small car around the garage. The difficult part was my feet and legs, it was still some time before I was to make any gains in that department. Obviously with all this relighting of the pathways within my brain it didn't lessen the trips to the CT scanner, but now I was able to put across my terror and dislike of this experience, but still I had to go through the emotional ordeal.

The next stage was of course going home, I vaguely remember the day apart from being lifted into the back of my dad's car. I can recall being outside of the hospital and visually I can place building structures, windows and fresh air. The next memory was the following morning with my parents lifting me from my bed and placing me on to my feet, instantly I fell to one side and went down on to the floor. I can recall that moment like it was yesterday, where things were in my bedroom, the texture of the carpet, but that thought I had of 'why am I on the floor?', 'why am I not stood up?', 'what's wrong', I can remember asking myself. It was the same feeling I had when I first came around after the accident, like being back at square one again, just utter pandemonium within my head. To think that the hospital had discharged me without being able to stand or walk, 'was this it for the rest of my life' I asked myself, had my parents been told that I may never walk again? It was really strange because I knew what the feeling was like; to walk, to move around and the sensation of standing up, but why wasn't I doing it. It's stated that when somebody has a limb removed for whatever the reason then your brain still has the perception that the limb is still there even though it isn't, for myself I had all the perception, still had my limbs, but it was the signals that were obviously not getting through.

Again, I had no idea right of time, but eventually movement and coordination started to return albeit in small stages. I spent a lot of time going backwards and forwards to hospitals for the likes of physiotherapy appointments and having to go through yet more uncomfortable and daunting experiences from tugging and prodding of my limbs to the CT scanning. Eventually came the day when I was able to put one foot in front of the other, easy as it sounds it was quite a task, it was obviously something that I hadn't done since before the accident so the feeling felt almost like a new experience. There were a lot of days and weeks where it felt like things were never happening. For my mum and dad on that day that I stood and took them first steps once again must have been just ridden with unimaginable joy and elation. Things didn't just stop there though, more physiotherapy followed for months after. Over time I had developed a shortening of the tendons in my legs in which my parents were offered different options that may assist me in the future, but were not guaranteed to be successful, these ranged from operations that would be quite intrusive which could have actually made things worse in the long run. One of the ideas was that I would be fitted with leg braces, they decided against any sort of medical procedure, but were advised that possible leg callipers should be the ones to try.

It was one afternoon at a place called Dorin Park just on the outskirts of Chester, it was a school, or a specialist place for people with disabilities, I think. It was just somewhere that I didn't want to be, for me it was filled with all the thoughts of terror and uncertainty, a really scary place, each time I was taken there I had an almost stomach wrenching feeling that I just wanted to run out of the place, the memories are that of pain and discomfort beyond anything that I have ever experienced since that point in my life, to use the word torturous would be unfair, but at the time it was just unbearable, so this one afternoon they needed to take a moulding of my legs to construct the calliper that would be fitted at a later date. I lay on this examination bed like you see in the doctor's room or in a hospital cubicle and they plaster casted my legs up which was the easy part and quite pleasant, but then once the plaster had set and the procedure to cut and remove the castings started, that's when my stresses began. At just five years old seeing that circular saw, and it being taken to within millimetres of the flesh on my bony legs was so terrifying that even today it gives me a spine-chilling feeling, but as I am sitting here now writing this I actually have a plaster cast on my arm following a broken wrist, so I will once again be reliving the circular saw memories in a few weeks' time with the removal of the cast.

After just a few weeks at home a lady turned up at the house for the appointment to fit the newly made calliper, on today's standards it was shit, made of a fleshy coloured hard plastic with a raised toe section to elevate the front of my foot, it boasted two straps on the front that ran across the shin area to hold it in place. It was horrific, the worst type of medical grade equipment you could possibly offer to a five-year-old child, putting it on for the first time was and is indescribable. Needless to say I never did wear it, it ended up in my dad's garage for years and I think at one point it was used as a holder for some tools until eventually it was thrown out, after just a few trials of the contraption it was just far too uncomfortable to wear.

So it was back to my daily physiotherapy programme that had been set out, but as a five-year-old that just longs to be in that comfort zone of toys and things to play with I soon started to refuse to do any of the exercises that had been suggested, mainly because they were uncomfortable, painful and with my mother and father being left to carry out these procedures on a daily basis you can only imagine how they must have felt. From seeing their first born lay by the roadside blood covered, to then living the day-to-day untold memories that they must have endured through my time in hospital to now be presented with having to carry out exercises on their son that feels pain and discomfort when doing the exercises, then says that he doesn't want to do them because they hurt, they never gave up, they always asked and advised that it would help me in the future, but I simply refused as I didn't want to feel any more pain.

So that was that, I started to blend back into the little boy that I used to be, playing out, doing the stuff that kids of the 80s did and enjoying myself, I had check-ups from time to time with the specialist and different appointments. The next big step was to ride a bike again, I recall being on the drive way at home, my dad pushing my bike out from the garage, it was the same bike that I was riding when the car hit me, I loved that bike, absolutely loved it! It was my cousin's before I got my hands on it, my dad had painted it in a bright green colour for the frame, the mudguards had been painted white, it had 10 inch wheels with white tires, white handlebar grips and white saddle, oh and not to forget the white rubberised peddles! It was just perfect in my eyes, a right little cruising dream, but that day he pushed it from the garage something happened, I no longer looked at this bike in the way that I did, I saw it as the thing that hurt me, the instrument that caused me mental and physical trauma. I stood there and cried, just the sheer site of this once wonderful machine of beauty that used to carry me round like a king with a sense of freedom was now just a horrible and inconceivable piece of metal that I never wanted to see again. I ran into the house and that was the last time I ever laid eyes on it.

The following Christmas I received a brand new BMX, fully chromed up with all the trimmings to go with it, I couldn't wait to hop on to it, though I was also feeling a little sceptical as to my ability to ride a bike again. I hadn't ridden since the accident a few years previous and even though I knew how to ride, 'could I actually do it' or was it to be like the whole walking and talking process of knowing but not being able to activate the signals along with the neurological pathways.

Well, on I got and off I went, my biggest struggle was my balance and coordination, I had no real space awareness, I was shit scared of riding in the road so what the hell was I doing! I mapped out a very small circuit in the street that was mainly riding on the pathway, I went round and round on that circuit getting faster each time! I must have looked really special to anyone passing or observing as I rode around in my own world, the sense of freedom was immense, well until I decked it on one of the grassy corners, and then mentally I was freaked out! That was me back at square one.

There's a saying that I've heard time and time again, that says it's not the amount of times that you fall down that makes you strong, but the amount of times that you can get knocked down, and keep getting back up. That definitely seemed to be the case on that day, also in the weeks that followed, in fact I still fall off the bike now! I think I was on the floor more times than I was on the bike, but I kept going back for more like I was enjoying it or something. The day came when I decided to venture out of the street, that day was a serious head fucker I can tell you, I remember the feeling of insurmountable anxiety mixed utter excitement, I mean what a rush of chemical delight that was! With riding on a path that I had never ridden before it was seriously outside of the comfort zone of riding around that circuit looking extra special from time to time, but like learning to walk again, unless you make that first step, then it isn't ever going to happen.

So there we go, I was mobile in every sense that you could be as a kid of the 80s, walking, and now riding a bike once again, I can't really say I felt lucky or different, I was just doing what every other kid was doing, I didn't really notice that I walked different to everyone else or that I had an arm that hung in odd positions, I just got on with it, no one pointed out the fact that I wasn't the same as all the other kids, things just took care of themselves, like I pointed out, the brain is just on automatic day and night, it delivers even if you don't ask it to, but if you put a question or a task to it then over time it will grow and the more you ask of it the more it will grow and develop…

Chapter 3
The FAM

As a kid I used to spend a lot of time with my dad both at home and in his place of work, health and safety wasn't what it is now. He was an HGV driver and at any given opportunity I would gladly join him on his travels around the country, even from the age of around two years old, I would sit in the passenger seat for hours, travelling around the country for two, three and even four days at a time, sleeping in the bunk bed behind the seats in my sleeping bag at night, just enjoying seeing different places. For years I did this, I think the very last time was when I was 17 years old. It made me happy, put a smile on my face. I also remember playing in the back garden at different stages, times spent in the paddling pool that we had at the time, no hot tubs back then! There were two brothers that lived two doors down from our house that my brother and I used to hang around with, we would dress up in camouflage gear, smear mud on our faces and take to the local woods where we would play for hours with sticks and other obscure items that we could use to play with pretending to be little solders scrabbling around in the trees and fields that our estate backed on to.

One particular day sticks in my mind, my brother came with us, we were climbing trees, it was wet. I remember saying to him as he was following me up this one tree that to watch the branches as they were slippery, then the next minute he fell, we didn't realise at that moment that he had in fact broken his arm, all we could think of was getting him back home, it was an arduous journey as we were deep in the undergrowth, dragging him up muddy wet inclines which were slippery, requiring everything we had as eight year olds, another time we thought we were sailors and that we could use a huge storage container as a raft without realising that physics was actually a thing, needless to say it didn't end well as we struggled to keep this thing balanced in the water of this stream, with the branches that we had collected before we boarded our ship to use as oars we quickly realised that we were in a world of bother when they were failing to establish any sort of coordination for us. Eventually the inevitable happened as the container capsized disappearing faster than a toupee in a hurricane beneath the water, leaving us with just the branches as a momentum of the day.

My brother Ryan and I with the look of guilt and mischief, like my second shadow always following me around.

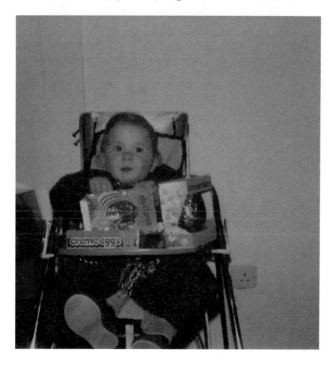

Chocolate buttons all the way even back then...

With just a very small unit to our family most of my young childhood was based around mum and dad and my younger brother Ryan, we would do everything together. I don't recall actually a lot before my accident, we have a lot of photos, but I can't remember any of the occasions or place a lot, well I say that, but I do have the occasional flashbacks, albeit very small, but they are quite significant. It's funny how our mind selects certain stages or occasions in our lives and logs them with a certain importance, I wasn't treated any different at home after my accident, well not in a way that I recall being different, I don't really remember any visits as such from health workers or specialist etc., only really the plastic leg fitting day, I mean there probably was. My brain after its knock was perhaps not really switched on to storing information.

New bikes and new jumpers, the cutting edge of 80s fashion, I honestly don't know what my brother had on his legs though...

So we lived in a suburb area of Chester, nothing like Hollyoaks or the house wives of Cheshire, it was around an 80/20% mix of council housing mixed in with private housing with the council housing taking up the majority of the area. We lived in a three-bedroom semi-detached house that was in one of the small pockets of the private housing areas. We weren't like posh, just your average street with working class families. The area itself was like rough and scary, sometimes you would get the feeling of being in a jungle and I felt quite vulnerable at times, my mum would sometimes ask me to go to the shop, instantly I would be thinking, *Shit! I'm actually going to die*, every corner that I turned would present some sort of danger, and on return you gained a sense of triumph that you had crossed the no man's land safely.

Travelling the country with my dad and my nappy before I could even talk.

Looking for mischief wherever I went even back then, seems to have been a trait that has stuck with me...

My very first bike, sneakily avoided stabilizers by going for 3 wheels to start.

We are quite a private family, keep ourselves to ourselves, my dad's side of the family were quite big with seven brothers and sisters in total, but we very rarely saw any of them when we were growing up as they all lost touch with each other over the years because they are scattered all over the place. My mother's side is a small number of four and again we never really saw anyone from that side. We spent a lot of time around at my nan's when myself and my brother were little, she was the closest just living around the corner, so she would either come around with sweets and the like and just spoil us as nans do after she had navigated the route through the streets. Whenever we went to hers, Ryan, my brother and I used to get all of her clean bedding out of the cupboards and use her clothes maid to make a den every time, she lived in a flat where the block was full of old folk that used to spoil the hell out of us with sweets as well, so we would be pretty much on a winner each time we went there. My mother's sister also lived just up the road which I remember us visiting, I must have been about seven or eight, I used to like going there as my cousin had a massive bedroom, all around the outside of it they had constructed a model Hornby train set with little towns with cars, tunnels and just some amazing bits of scenery. I remember that I would sit for hours watching the trains go around this landscape almost in a dream of a make believe land, the sounds and the smell of a train set are just unique, imagining that I was miniature within the streets of the model set itself with its suspension bridge at the far end of the room and major town at the opposite end. I could sit in the middle of the room and have a panoramic view as the trains would pass each other at different locations each time as one travelled faster than the other, a calming feeling as the sunlight would beam through the window, reflect on the tiny windows in the buildings and the trains themselves as they passed swiftly, I would dream for hours, I wished that somehow I could live in them villages and play near the little stream that ran under the suspension bridge and then guided itself in and around the villages before slowly disappearing behind one of the hills that had been constructed to give the effect of an endless horizon. At some point in the 80s my mum's sister and family packed up and disappeared to Australia never to be seen again. They sold the train set to some collector and that was the last that I saw of it, and them as well to be honest, since then I have always wanted my own model train set, but have never really had the space or the time to construct one, maybe one day when I'm not riding a bike. So with my closest auntie gone we just had my nana; well, there was my dad's mum and dad, they also lived around the corner, but things for me and my brother just didn't feel the same for them as we did for my mum's mum, they smoked heavily and their house just stank like really bad, they were also quite abrupt with us two; did we ever do anything wrong, but I suppose with them having brought up seven kids of their own in a suburb of London through probably some of the most difficult times during the 1940s I should think that maybe their discipline towards their own kids was quite harsh, but that's only a guess, they also had a dog that used to climb all over me and bark which I didn't like. I was always one to be chased by dogs so I wasn't that into them, I think a fear had developed at some point that I couldn't get out of my head, when it barked because of my involuntary body movements due to my disability it would cause my spasms to kick off. So, yeah, the relationship just wasn't really there, I mean we would never jump for joy when it was mentioned that we were going around to see nanny and granddad, it was more of a: "oh let's put on our dirty clothes because you were either going to be leaving there covered in dog hair or smelling like an ash tray, we would leave there with sore throats from inhaling the passive smoke that would take a day at least to get over, I kid you not. In a way we wanted things to be different, we did accept them for who they were, but we never really took to them, maybe we just didn't feel the same love and stuff that we got from our other man and our parents. Quite sad really.

In 1991, my mum's mum flew out to see my aunt in Australia, but became quite ill while she was out there and passed away whilst trying to get back to the UK, it was as you can imagine quite a traumatic time for my mum and dad, I can't remember much. I suppose a child's understanding of someone passing isn't that of an adult so my brother and I just kind of carried on going to school and stuff. After that point the family became just us four, we still had my dad's parents that we would see from time to time but we definitely felt the effect of my nan not being there. My dad was in and out of work doing this and doing that, he was an HGV driver by trade, he would work for different people from time to time, I think it was a case of when they had work then he would go and do a bit, I don't think he was full-time employed because he seemed to be home a lot as well, but that could have just been my odd sense of time, maybe he was, but I just didn't realise it. He also went through a spell of running his own business as a painter and decorator, but again I'm unsure it wasn't actually a legitimate business as one minute he was driving lorries, and the next he was painting somebody's house, I mean the chances of him being registered with the inland revenue had to be a slim chance. I mean don't quote me on that, but from what I know now about him it was probably all cash in hand, a bit of a real life Del Boy. He himself came from the Shepherd's Bush area of London so the flyboy mentality was already in him from a young age I think, always cutting some sort of deal. I remember his favourite saying wherever us kids would ask where he was going, he would just reply with a quick and loud "see a man about a dog". I would often think that he was 'actually ' going to come home with a pet dog for us, in a way that would scare me each time he said it, I would fret all day and night thinking that he would turn up after one of his many outings with the biggest most terrifying dog ever, fortunately that wasn't the case, but what was happening to these so-called dogs that he was going to see about, was he a secret pet dealer, a real life doctor Doolittle or was it more the fact that he never wanted to actually tell us where he was off to. Looking back now maybe it was some dodgy deal or maybe it was just another cash in the hand job that he had stumbled upon, well whatever it happened to be it kept us two boys fed, watered and clothed which was the main thing. He would do anything for us two boys, we never really wanted for much, well it seemed that way, I'm sure there were many times when we were on our arse as they say, but my dad weathered it, we were not well off, always had a different car every couple of months, what that was about I will never know, they were all old bangers. I remember we had a mini, but the estate version, a clubman I think they call it, the back doors were just about secured to the back of the car by a thin layer of rust, each time we went out in it you could small the exhaust fumes venting through the back doors. We went on holiday once to North Wales, during the journey my dad had to stop as us two lads had fallen asleep on the back seat from inhaling the what was 4-star leaded petrol gases back then, 'yeah, highly dangerous' I hear you thinking, death defying to be honest. Perhaps had my dad have not stopped then we may not be here today; great my dad, always thinking of our health and looking after us on what was such a long car trip. We had that particular car for a number of years until we upgraded to something that had an MOT and was a bit bigger and with seals around the doors but it still only had two doors. I remember all my friends' parents in the street that I knew all had cars with four doors which I associated as family cars. Us, we had the bachelor type run around for a family of four, always struggling for space and always feeling cooped up in the back with my brother that would suffer car sickness on even the shortest of journeys, not even having your own window to roll down as my brother was about to throw up was a sort of small problem as he quite often had to lean over and squeeze his head between the back of the front passenger chair and the front side window to stick his head out to be sick as we were moving along the road, quite often leaving the side of the car a homing beacon for flies and the like to follow. I recall one year my parents being forward thinking and purchasing some anti travel sickness pills for him, this lead to a somewhat more than interesting trip to North Wales as they had some sort of ingredient in them which coursed him to hallucinate, so they had cured the being sick out of the window, but now he wanted to climb out as he thought that he could fly, I recall it lasting hours, and once we had return home the doctor was called to see if there was anything that he could do only to be greeted by my brother thinking that he was seeing people inside of the cupboards and running around as high as a kite, my brother obviously had the best trip ever that weekend.

My mother was a housewife, choosing to stay at home and looking after the family was back then the normal thing for a mother and wife to do. A lot of families in the street were the same, my mother would wake us in the mornings, take us to school, return home and deal with the daily running of the home. I recall her baking, cooking, cleaning and whatever else was necessary to run a tight ship. I think that is where I have gotten a little bit of my cleanliness from along with the discipline that I learnt during my professional cycling career with regards to looking after your equipment, keeping your kit clean and organised. It is, I think, a very important attribute to have as it can also keep your mind tidy and organised, which again is imperative when training and competing at a high level. I was always turned out in clean clothes and scrubbed up well whenever we had to go anywhere of any significance. We just led a normal life like everyone else, there wasn't anything that was outrageous about the way we lived in the respect that we didn't have exclusive flamboyant holidays or have designer clothes. There was no pressure to have the latest up to the minute toys or computer games. Life was just simple, well through my eyes anyway, maybe if I asked my mother and father, they may say different. So we lived in this street for about three years, then moved just around the corner into a bungalow, it was tiny, a two bedroom and very old, but had a massive garden with two lawns, a vegetable patch and a greenhouse. I sound a right geek now but I learnt to grow food in the years that we lived there which actually won me a gardeners badge at Cubs, yeah that's Cubs as in a neckerchief and a cap… Boba job and all of that shebang… Again, it was a way to learn things, to develop my interpersonal skills, get myself active and build on my disciplines. Since obviously the accident which was by now six years earlier, I was still behind all my peers at school and struggled a lot to interact on the same level as my friends, I was immature for my age, but was that down to the accident or just a natural process, by becoming part of the Cubs was something that did help me a lot, I was interacting with kids other than those I went to school with and those of different ages which moved me on a lot. It increased my self-esteem and gave me more confidence to take part in stuff that I wouldn't normally do, it brought me out of myself a little more each time I attended on a Monday evening, and then when there was ever an outing to a different environment, again it would broaden my horizons more. Though I recall one particular weekend we had been roped into doing the obligatory shoeshine outing at the local supermarket, there was just two of us that had been selected to do this. Apparently it was of great prestige to do this particular deed in the cub movement, if I am honest I didn't see the attraction, on my knees all day whilst people poked their feet at you armed with a brush and a rag, tough going really, I didn't even get a badge for it, and where did all the money go: I'll tell you, on the new conservatory that the Arkala was having built at his house, that's where. I mean who was there to oversee the goings on, I mean I didn't see any improvements at the scout hut, well it wasn't even that, it was a room at a small church up the road from where I lived, and for all the funds that were raised through different events that we did year after year we never actually gained our own hut, I was only in it for the cap and neckerchief any way.

I turned down the option to go on to the scouts once the Cubs had come to an end, it all seemed a bit regimented, and there are only so many badges that you can collect before it becomes boring, I mean one badge just looked like another, and my jumper was looking a bit like a patchwork quilt.

By the age of 12 or 13 my interests were starting to develop, cars and different outside influences were taking a hold, I used to travel with my dad a lot in his line of work on most of the school holidays so it broadened my knowledge of the country, plus it gave me lots of thinking time just sat in the passenger seat of his truck going up and down the country for days on end.

I was never really a mad sporty active child, we did a sponsored run during my primary school years for the band aid movement at the time, I think it was 1985 or 86 that we did this run, it was on the school field around the running track and was based on the amount of laps that you completed. I ran around this track with a different teacher on each lap, for some reason they wouldn't let me run alone, perhaps they thought that I was a high risk or special in some way or another, so there I was being treated differently to all the other kids that were running around that day. I recall running with one of the teachers and her asking me as we were running if I was OK. As I turned my head and looked up to answer her, her eyes were crossed, she was sweating profusely, and had no coordination whatsoever as a runner. I wanted to ask her if she was in fact OK, but as the little dot that I was I just kept my thoughts to myself, but honestly she did not look in the best of health, and perhaps she should not have taken part on that day.

So growing up over the next few years, going through puberty and adolescence was a tricky time, that fight of the inner child and the adult hormones was difficult to deal with, all my friends had in my eyes accelerated in front of me. I felt that I was been left behind in this respect, but I also didn't feel ready to go to this next stage of life yet, it felt too soon, but I knew I needed to act differently around my friends through fear of being cast to one side because of my childlike acts etc. One day I would wake up feeling like I wanted to take on the world as a grown up, then other days would be like I just wanted to play with my toy cars, or get my box of Lego down and waste the day dreaming whilst building. We have all been there at different stages of our childhoods, some seem to handle it better than others. Me, I don't think I have ever come out of that stage or ever will. My brother was growing up faster than myself I would say, I noticed that he was doing things that were beyond my years; this sort of worried me slightly. I was confused to where I was really, but that then begged the question 'Was I ever going to grow out of those childlike tendencies?' or are they likely to be very much a part of me. Maybe it's a comfort thing that subconsciously wants to still be present. People say that men never grow up, that they are like big kids, but the strange thing is, 'it's true', I used to think people were joking or taking the piss when they made comments about me being a child etc., even my mother calls me Peter Pan. I understand the 'roles' of an adult, but struggled to get to grips with it; but does it actually matter? Life is too short. I suppose it's fully down to you as an individual whether you want to take on the whole grown up way of life. I deal with enough stresses on a daily basis anyway so why would I want to add to that. I don't know really, it's all very confusing, maybe I just analyse things too much rather than just going with it. See, I'm actually in a debate with myself now, I can't win…

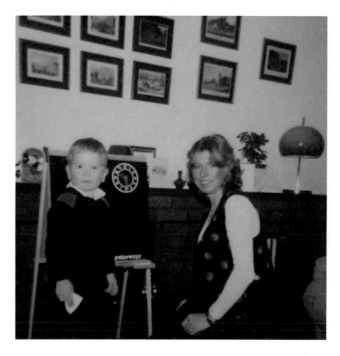

My Mother always teaching me, even today I learn something new from her each time we speak.

Always setting a trend even at preschool aged just 3.

My brother and I always digging holes whether in sand or mud,
even today I seem to dig holes that I struggle to get out of...

So as the years ticked by the family interactions altered slightly, my mother and father were showing signs of not getting on and finding it hard to live together. They always seemed that they would never be the ones to break up and divorce like the rest of the extended family had done over the years. My brother was the first to leave home and eventually got married to Nikki, this left myself at home with two parents that just weren't getting on. My dad was still in his driving job but approaching the end of his working life. I was 24 years old, still at home having just signed my professional contract as a bike rider when my dad was diagnosed with lymphoma, a type of blood cancer. I had just returned from a competition in Switzerland and went straight to visit him in the hospital where he had just undergone an operation to remove his spleen, I couldn't really take in what was being explained about the illness or the outcome. The doctors gave him a life expectancy of five to seven years following intense chemotherapy, again this was completely unimaginable and we all struggled to understand it. I can't say I was shocked or stunned because I just didn't understand. In the following months he went from the big strong figure that I knew was my dad to a weakened shadow of a human being, a scary unimaginable process, but this was medication that was supposedly making him better, I couldn't get my head around it. As more time passed he had to take early retirement from his work due to ill health, at this point things became a lot more difficult, he would be at home a lot with no or very little energy to do anything, it was hard to go about the daily routine of training, and any other stuff that we had to do. My mum was affected in a way that I had never seen her before, suddenly the prospect of my dad not being around was becoming more and more realistic as the years ticked by. He started drinking heavily which started to take its toll even more on their relationship, I tried to blank out and ignore what was going on but living in the same house it was hard to avoid. I remember just sitting in my bedroom, hearing the arguments and witnessing the sometimes-unbearable atmosphere that they had created between them, to which I just had to absorb as I had nowhere else to go. In 2005, I met Natalie and in 2006 I moved out of the family home to go and live with her in Manchester in our own place. I didn't know how this was going to leave things with my mum and dad, they obviously weren't getting along together pre the cancer diagnosis and over the past few years it had been extremely difficult for them both, but at least I had been there to ease things a little doing what I could, whereas now I wasn't. I could have stayed at home forever. I carried some sort of guilt and anticipation as to what now was going to happen. The following year after talks with the doctor my dad decided that he wanted to go and live in Spain for a while, as it was something that he had always wanted to do, and now with the prospect of his life not being as long as he had hoped my mum and dad separated and went their own ways. It was a difficult time for everyone, I never envisioned my parents breaking up, I don't think anyone at any age imagines that happening to their parents, but unfortunately it happens and it's never an easy time. It had been coming for a long time and I noticed it when I was living at home a few years earlier, they just weren't getting on at all, arguing all the time and stuff. So they sold the family home, my mother

39

found an apartment in Chester itself as she didn't really want to move from the city that she had lived in for so many years. My dad found a place in Spain down on the southeast coast close to Murcia, he was happy for sure, and I think in the end my mum was better off as she had her own space. They didn't file for divorce as they both didn't feel the need to, it was more a case that they just couldn't live together anymore. So with the Paralympic games approaching I was fearing the worst, he had undergone countless treatments of chemotherapy which had been stabilising the cancer, but we were approaching the seven-year prediction that the doctors had first calculated. It was 2008, my now sister-in-law Nikki was pregnant with my brother's first child, amazing that our family unit was going to gain a new edition, but all my thoughts were on the fact of the doctors telling my dad all them years back about their life expectancy being just seven years maximum, but also that they now had the cancer under some sort of control, that they have no indication as to life expectancy and with him feeling much better than what he was a few years earlier I didn't know what to think. Was this good news, or just a false way that cancer can present itself; he seemed all good and was getting on with things in Spain, coming back for his test appointments etc., so things in general where reaching some sort of normality, but I was still very apprehensive. In September of 2008, the whole family including my dad flew out to the Beijing Paralympic Games to watch me compete. It was amazing that my dad had gone through almost eight years of treatment and that he was able to see me gain my first Paralympic medal. Nikki had just giving birth a few months before the games so was unable to fly out with little Alfie, but I had a photo of him that I took to the podium with me to receive my medal, it was a special moment for the whole family as my dad was there to enjoy and see the moment I was handed the medal, as according to the doctors back in 2001, technically he wasn't predicted to be here at this time.

For the next few years his condition stabilised itself with the treatment and all seemed OK in 2010 we had another addition to the family from my brother a week before my marriage to Natalie; just again amazing, this time it was a girl, they called her Florence. I was to become a godfather for the second time. Not being a dad myself I love spending time with Alfie and Florence, it gives me the excuse to be the big kid and just embrace the time with them. Perhaps one day I may get the chance to have some of my own, who knows eh…

So as the next Paralympic Games in 2012 was just around the corner my dad caught some sort of an infection whilst back in the UK on a family visit. With having no spleen, he is very susceptible to bugs and the like, more than say me and you. He was on massive amounts of medication to combat this, but some bugs are known to get through and then cause a secondary infection which can be the killer. It happened very quickly in the way that it took hold, within a few hours he was in hospital where the doctors wanted to put him in an induced coma. This was in the April of 2012, I remember rushing down the motorway that evening because they didn't think that he had long as the infection had turned to pneumonia which in a healthy person can be life threatening so for my dad it was literally knocking on the gates. I had a million thoughts going through my head as I drove down the motorway: my first and foremost thought was would I get to the hospital in time, I don't recall looking at the dial on the dim lite dashboard, but all I can tell you is that I travelled the 50 or so miles from where we lived up in Lancashire to Chester in just over 30 minutes. When I arrived, the doctors were very eager to put him in this coma as quickly as possible. They took us to one side and said in no simpler terms that we should go and see him before he is placed in the coma. This only meant one thing, they stressed for us to expect the worst. I remember being sat there, I was listening but it just wasn't sinking in the enormity, and just at how final this could be. I didn't know what to say, I looked around and my mum was in tears, so too were my brother and Natalie, but for some reason I was not. Was it the shock at what I had just been told or what, I just didn't know how to react, I was struggling to find any emotion inside of me, I had felt the need to travel to the hospital quickly because I was obviously feeling something, but then once there, and from hearing what the doctors had told us I was now feeling nothing. It is the worst feeling ever, feeling that I should be showing feelings for what is actually going on, but there I was just numb and unfazed, well that's how it seemed. This was my dad, lying there, on the absolute brink of breathing his last, and I had no emotion. As the doctors finished saying what they said we then had to go see him before they took him to induce the coma, I remember walking through the small A and E ward that he was on and into the cubicle where he was. My brother instantly hugged him whilst trying to hold back the tears, I could see that he was clearly distort and was struggling with things, my dad just lay there, not really knowing what was going on, nor saying a lot. He seemed in an almost confused state by the situation, one because of the way that the infection was attacking his system, but also with the strong drugs that he had obviously been given on arrival at the hospital. I felt like I was removed from the situation, almost an onlooker with no connection. My brother left the room, and I was left stood there, a moment's hesitation. I was lost in my mind as to what to say or do, I was digging deep for answers into an open void, surely I had 'something'… Eventually I moved towards him and placed my arm around his withered shoulders: I muttered something, but I can't remember what, as I left the cubical I turned and looked at him, his head down confused like, I recall that I thought it would be my last memory and vision of him. I took another pace forward, I stopped, turned and took a second look, and whispered "See you, Dad", but still I had no emotions, tears or the deep stomach sickness that I would have expected to feel in such a traumatic situation.

I returned to the room where my brother and mother were, they were both in tears, my brother stood up and hugged me whilst flooded in tears and emotion, I threw my arms around him to console him, we stood there, him sobbing like I had never witnessed before. I glanced over his shoulder to see my mum sat in a chair in the same distraught manner, I was unsure what to do at this point, still trying to deal and comprehend my own non-emotional state whilst trying to ease theirs. By now the doctors had left to go about their business in stabilising my dad. As the time passed and other people's tears became less, logical thinking had made itself present. It was by now quite late, but I made the decision to call my dad's younger sister as they still kept in touch with each other from time to time, and with the doctors preparing us for the worst I made the call. To give someone some difficult news at 2 am in the morning is not something that I have ever done before; it was quite a surreal moment. Straight away she said that she would come up, my aunt lives 300 miles away, but did not hesitate for a second. Within a few hours she arrived with her family. Later that morning we were all taken into a room by the doctors and medical staff, they told us that my dad was now under the medically induced coma and that this would be his and their best chances of dealing with all the issues that have so quickly festered from the initial infection that he had picked up. They stressed that he was extremely poorly and to prepare ourselves for the worst, again everyone in the room were in tears and finding things too much to handle, yet I still couldn't understand why I didn't seem to be grasping the enormity of the situation.

I have never really been a person to deal with illness very well, more in a sense that when I'm ill I just tend to get on with things rather than make a big deal out of it, but here we were with the scale of what was going on and again I just didn't seem engaged with it. Was I subconsciously refusing to accept that I may lose my dad, or was it more a case of thinking that it will blow over and all be OK, or like everything else in my life was I just drifting through. Within a few days they had moved my dad to an intensive care unit within the hospital, he was at high risk of more infection but the staff were doing everything possible to minimise this from happening.

After taking a few days off training to sort things out at home and with the family I made the decision to return to the track and resume training. A training camp was planned at the London track where trials would be held for selection for the Paralympic Games so any more time away from training may have affected any chance that I may have had of my qualification spot, and I knew somehow that my dad wouldn't have wanted me to miss out just because he was lay in some hospital bed with tubes sticking out of him to keep him alive. As the weeks ticked by there was little or no change in my dad's health. The machines were keeping him alive and the drugs were fighting the infections, it was hard going to see him as we would just sit there for hours, no one really saying anything. The sounds of the air pump that was feeding his lungs and the different beeps that would go off every so often to indicate if the saline solution needed changing or the feed bag was empty, they were hard times in the sense that you felt helpless. Not able to talk to him or even just offer a facial expression had he been awake, there was nothing for a few months, but he was alive, the point arrived where the doctors wanted to try and bring him off of the life support to see if he could begin to regain control of his body. It would be a slow process in which I think the first two times were unsuccessful, but on the third attempt he did respond.

So by now he was awake, but not really with things; he still had the tracheostomy tube in to help him with his breathing and was still wired for food intake and saline so was still unable to communicate with us, plus his hearing had been affected by being in a coma, so our frustrations almost doubled even though he was awake we had no way of communicating. By now I had qualified a place for the London Paralympic Games and we just had around three months until the games themselves started in the September. To stay focused on my own performance over the past few months had been difficult. Chris Furber my coach at the time had been so understanding of the situation right from the beginning which really helped me stay focused in such a turbulent time. I was backwards and forwards to the hospital in Chester every other day straight after training, trying to cover anything that needed doing that involved the family. My dad still had his place in Spain that we were also trying to sort out because obviously he wasn't going to be going back there for a while or if at all, so we needed to make a decision on what to do. All his belongings were there and we just didn't know how long it was going to be before he could regain his speech or any understanding of communicating with us. Over all of that time I was also analysing myself, I was having deep thoughts and waking in the night asking myself why I was emotionless to all what had and was happening, why hadn't I cried like everyone else, why was I treating it like it was something that happen on a daily basis, why was I not caring about the situation, but I struggled to find the answers that I was looking for. I would listen to music from way back from when I was younger to try and rekindle some of the early memories of my dad, the good times and the times that he came to my rescue if I was ever hurt. It took me a long time searching, but then surely these feelings should be natural. You shouldn't have to go in search of them? Was I that cold? Had I not got feelings? I started to ask myself, and if I did, what had happened for them to be buried so deep that they had to be forced out.

By July 2012, my dad was at a point where the doctors were happy to discharge him from hospital as he was in full control of his body after the treatment and physiotherapy needed after spending such a long period of time laying in bed. The doctors were saying it's a complete miracle from where he had been the night that they induced him to now. After a few weeks staying with my mum at her apartment, he made the decision that he wanted to go back to Spain and would pop backwards and forwards for appointments and the like. At first we were all very sceptical about it as now his system was weaker than before so there was more risk to him catching an infection, and should he pick something up whilst in Spain there would be no one there should something take a hold as quick as it did last time. He is a pretty strongminded person and was adamant that this is what he wanted, we had to respect his wishes so off he went.

Of course, we were all very concerned for his health, but when my dad gets something in his mind, he just does it no matter how difficult or what obstacles are placed in the way. I suppose that is maybe where I get my drive from, so that was it, he said that he would be back for the games in the September and off he went.

For the next couple of months I couldn't comprehend why I felt no emotion during that period, different family members had formed their opinion and I would get it in the neck as to why I didn't care, but I did, but why did I not show it in a way that everyone else did, was I just unfazed or was I not seeing what others were, and understanding the importance of what the family were going through, or was I just that damn selfish that I didn't give a shit. This would bowl over in my mind for months afterwards, I would listen to that same music that I downloaded while he was in hospital trying to find some kind of emotion. People say that music and smells can bring back memories and place you in that exact space in time, but again I was finding nothing, I felt ashamed that I couldn't even draw on a moment in time that I could hold on to, to remember him by had he passed away that evening. The guilt and anguish I felt about myself was unbearable, my dad that's looked after me through my childhood, has seen me lay in the road bleeding helplessly after my accident, watched as I went through rehabilitation, has picked me up each time I fell, has saved me from drowning in the sea off the coast of Spain back in 1992 with total disregard for his own safety, someone that I could rely on and that would do anything for me regardless of what it was, yet in his time of need I couldn't emotionally connect with him, and felt a total outsider to what was going on, but this was only the beginning. As time went on I started to feel even more detached from him and everyone else, it's a horrible thought and even when I started to dig into my growing up and my emotional development I couldn't find at any stage that I may have had a difficult experience, or maybe suffered some sort of emotional isolation from my parents that may have manifested by lack of sharing of emotions. Both my mother and father showed both us boys affection, and we are of a loving home, but obviously somewhere along the line I have become disconnected from my own emotions.

As the next few years passed his condition was up and down, the doctors were keeping things under control with chemotherapy treatment.

As a family, well! since my brother and I left home really, we have never been ones to sit down as a family and talk about things. Natalie used to tell me that I was really bad for that, getting things out in the open and stuff. I tend to try and deal with it on my own, work things out and stuff.

At the end of 2015, my dad had to return to the UK because his health was at a stage where he was having to return a lot for hospital appointments, and logistically it just wasn't working for him living in Spain. It was a massive move which he didn't really want to make but didn't really have a choice as he knew his health was more important, the family had their own opinions on him moving back and we had to find somewhere for him that was suitable for his needs, this was the point where my disconnection really showed as I wanted nothing to do with it. In between all of this my dad had questioned to the doctors and specialist why I was so disconnected, even more now! After his time on the life support back in 2012, I think he had obviously been struggling with the fact that I wasn't as emotionally connected with him and that in his eyes I was a totally different person to how I was before. After much discussion the specialists came to the conclusion that I had grieved for him during the weeks and months of the coma, as I was told that he was very ill at the time and that the doctors weren't expecting him to pull through, but obviously he did which left me in a confused state subconsciously and consciously. This kind of made sense to me, but I still don't know why at the time I didn't show any emotion. The hardest thing was trying to understand the Unknown. I love my mum and dad and maybe the emotional side of things will all come out one day, they say that when you least expect it, things happen. I don't know where I'm at now, I can only think that all my emotions, love and passion have been devoted to my sport from such a young age that I know of no other way to channel them, and with doing so has left me not being able to associate feelings with anything other than what I feel when I'm riding or racing a bike. It doesn't excuse that fact that in the face of others that it may seem that I am being a complete bastard. I just don't know anything else, or I did, but have lost my way many years ago and have been unable to pull things back because all I have seen is what I have been aiming at.

Over the last 12 months since 2017 my dad's health has taken a turn for the worst, he is very hard of hearing, has lost all but most of his sight and is none too good on his legs through what the doctors have described as mini strokes. My emotions have changed slightly, not as much as I would have liked, but things are better than they were, I now pick up the phone to call him, I visit him a lot, and do as much as I can for him, I look at things now in a way that I viewed my father from such a young age as the person that would do everything, that person that would never give up come hell or high water. When he became ill I did grieve for him in my own way, when someone of a doctor's knowledge and experience is stood in front of you basically informing you in not as many words that you need to prepare yourself for the worst, then that's what you do. I don't believe in luck or live in hope, I never have done and never will do so when you are faced with that scenario you just get on with it, and that's what I did. Hard or as selfish as it may sound it's the truth, I still feel the same way toward him, but I suppose with him now being unable to be that person that could do everything, the person that I viewed as my hero when I was younger then it now is my time to step in and do what I can and maybe this is the way my emotions work because I sure don't know any other way.

Chapter 4
School Scars

The time eventually came for me to return to school after my accident, it was something that I hadn't really thought about in all the time that had passed. I suppose for any child it's all about the here and now and not about what's going to happen two, three or even five years down the line. The primary school that I had attended from around the age of four years old was a small school catering for a population of no more than around 170 kids at maximum from the local area. It was surrounded by a yellow fence, and the front of the two-storey building was a patchwork design of different coloured panels that obviously the architect had used elsewhere, as I recall seeing other buildings within the area with the same pattern and design of brickwork even down to the smallest of detail with the plant pots and door handles.

Just before my return to school I received a huge A3 sized blue paper folder with cards and pictures from all of the other kids both in my class and other classes in school wishing me well and that they were looking forward to seeing me again. I still have this folder now and all of the contents that I received 36 years ago, it's strange when I look over the cards and pictures because it takes me right back to that part of my life almost instantaneously with no hesitation, I mean just how powerful is the brain to do that, it just amazes me each time, to give you the exact feeling at any moment that you choose across anything that you have done in your life. I think a lot about my past and different points, things that I have done and my schooling especially is a poignant moment in my life that I hold close to me in the sense that it was a new starting point after my accident filled with joyful times and memories that I cherish especially on the primary level, not so much the high school level which I will talk about later on.

So there I was, back in the fold, back doing what every kid does Monday to Friday; getting dragged out of my bed, dressing up in a lacklustre grey uniform, white shirt and a red and black striped tie and having to squeeze my jittery feet into footwear that was non-forgiving with their pointed toe shaped design as that was the school's protocol with no exceptions.

On an academic level I struggled right the way through education as my brain just would not absorb the information at the rate that it was being educated to me, I would listen and write stuff down, albeit at a slow rate, but I struggled with containing the information due to fatigue, so would just switch off and drift into my own world. We would do PE a few times a week which is where I would encounter my first big challenging situations, for instance the school had apparatus frames that the others kids would set up at the start of the lesson and all get to play on and climb, whereas I just had to sit and watch on most occasions unless it evolved playing dead lions on a mat as the teacher didn't want me climbing. The feelings as I sat there watching everyone else having fun was that of isolation, rejection and frustration, even when we went out on to the field to play football I can remember never really being passed the ball or really included in the games. Even though health and safety weren't as in your face back then, I sense that even that wasn't the case. It was more the fact that I was noticeably different to the other kids at school level and therefor the teachers left me out because I was either to slow or just basically shit at stuff, which left them struggling to comprehend what to do with me, so they created this barrier that ended up travelling around with me wherever I went or whatever I wanted to take part in.

There were a few dare I say naughty kids in the class, not horrendous, but just mischievous and would test the teachers' patience each day as kids do, The head teacher Mrs Lynch, a hardened redhead that travelled 100 miles round trip from where she lived in North wales to school in Chester each day, would wear green most days of the week, either because she only had the one outfit, or because she wanted to complement her almost orange coloured hair that scared myself as I recall her looking very much like a witch that I had seen in a book that lived on one of the shelves in the classroom. So each time I had to encounter her all I could think of was this book and the story line of her casting a spell. She ran a really tight ship in the school and anyone that crossed her would be in for it, a few of the kids would be constantly in and out of her office to which you could hear her shouts and bellowing cantankerous voice travel down the corridors of the small school whenever she was cooking one of the kids. On one or two occasions I ended up on the wrong side of her humour and would be marched to her office while she was holding my ear, yes that's right, ear; don't mess with Lynchy was the motto amongst us kids back then.

Her office was just as scary as her, not only had you just had to listen to her yelling at you en route while trying to keep your head raised on one side as she gripped your ear by two of her bony fingers with her pointed nails digging into you, just to try and relieve some of the pressure that she was applying, then on entry to the office right in front of you as the door swung open was a full-sized hanging skeleton, a stark reminder that possibly someone someday did not get out alive, a really scary thought to the eight to nine year old that I was at the time. Once in the office the smell of two or three-day-old cigarettes lingered from around the glass ash tray that sat upon her desk, you knew you were in for it by the way that she threw herself back in her chair and crossed her legs to show her authority trying to unnerve you to the point of crying.

Even today I don't really understand what her beef was about, did she just enjoy shouting, did she have some sort of hang up about her own mixture of DNA which resulted in her orange hair and fiery personality, or like myself had she experienced a traumatic time as a child which left her scarred with anger. Of course there was lots of great times in primary as well, I enjoyed drawing and creating things from paper and card, which the school had to have some left-handed scissors ordered in especially for me which these days is pretty standard in any school, but it made me feel somewhat looked after 'if that makes sense'. I went on many trips out with my classmates to places like the zoo, the annual trip to the theatre at Christmas time and one in particular trip that stands out was in year six; it was a week in London staying with different families. I had been paired up with a classmate to stay with one family for the week for our accommodation. During the day we would meet up with our other classmates, see the sights and attractions that London had to offer and all the boring stuff. It was to be my first time away from home and without my family, so that being alone was a daunting thought. The coach journey down to London took what seemed like forever, but we seemed to be entertained at the fact there was a toilet on board of the coach and all of the boys would form a toilet train just to flush the loo. I don't know why we did that, perhaps it was the fact that we had never seen a toilet on a moving vehicle before and just had a vision of a huge spray of discoloured water heading out of the back of the coach and hitting the cars behind at each flush, like a sketch from a cartoon or a comic at the time.

The first port of call en route to our accommodation on the first day was a visit to Wembley stadium, that's the old one for anyone younger than me reading this. Armed with my Kodak 110 camera we did the tour, just a field of grass really, nothing really stood out for me, I wasn't really into football back then. Looking back and recalling the pictures that I took that day of bazaar things such as goal posts, a row of seats and the back of someone's head who wasn't even part of our group it dawned on me that I wasn't really interested in the touristy things that others seemed to become excited about. The days before the selfie, I do recall a number of times turning the camera around to take a picture of myself, but those were obviously the prints that when you received them back from the developers were of just sky or a rather over enthusiastic close up of your chin or forehead…

From there we went on to meet up with all the parents that would be looking after us in the evenings for the next week. As we all waited with anticipation at what would be awaiting us and as all the other kids were picked up and slowly dispersed of into the London suburban jungle, myself and my school buddy were the last ones left in this car park with a teacher. Eventually through some means of communication we proceeded to another location where we waited yet some more time to be collected, we were stood outside of a takeaway on a busy London street, there was a laundrette to the right hand side of the takeaway where a blonde woman appeared carrying a basket full to the brim with clothing and a fag hanging from her mouth. Yes! this was to be the lady that was to look after us for the next week. I cannot remember for the life of me what her name was, being just 10 years old I hadn't really formed much awareness of things, so I just went along with stuff and thought nothing of it. Compared to today's standards I look at it now and think that it was all so innocent, but at the same time it was also very slapdash, but back then it was like no one actually knew much, I don't know, maybe it was just me.

So eventually my classmate and I were bundled into the back of this car, and off we went, I couldn't tell you where in London that we were staying, only that it was in a block of flats in a somewhat rough looking area with boarded up buildings and the like. I had impressions of areas around where I lived that you just wouldn't stray into, and this looked like one of them so I was shitting myself! On first impression of the accommodation, well it was dark, dingy and small, it was top floor so the view of the rest of the estate was good from a point of view that you'd be able to see any trouble before venturing out! The lady had an older son and a baby that just cried nonstop for the whole week that we were there. For my first time away from home I was so very nervous and didn't feel comfortable. The sleeping arrangements were that of bunk beds to which I took the bottom as my classmate wanted the top.

The son of this woman was around 16 or 17, and after a few days started to talk, took us to the local park in the evenings and stuff like that for things to do rather than be cooped up in a small flat with a screaming baby. There was no sign of a dad unless he worked away. A few days into staying there the boy started showing myself and my class mate some undesirable adult magazines that were in this bedroom where we were sleeping to which we were obliviously not accustomed to. I can't find the words that I felt when this happened. I was 10 years old; until that point I was unaware of any such things, but for the rest of the time we were there it was on my mind that he would each evening have those magazines out. It was something that happened, I can't turn the clock back, I wished it had never happened. Nothing ever came of it, we didn't really understand at the time, I mean who does at 10 years old. It shouldn't have happened, the boy was obviously showing off that he had these magazines or they were somebody else's and he thought that he was being funny, boasting his masculinity or something, but it is was terrifying, that type of thing leaves a lasting image that you never really forget, and from that point on the trip I felt that my innocence as a small child had changed slightly. I didn't feel safe, I didn't say anything to the teachers for absolute fear, one! That the boy would have ended up in trouble, two! He knowing it was one of us boys that had said something which could have made things very awkward, I just tried to forget about it. For the rest of the stay I slept in my clothes, scared and worried about what I had seen, I recall the other kids would comment on me sleeping in my clothes after my classmate started to make reference to it, but I didn't care, it just felt the right thing to do. Today, and even writing this down it makes me feel sick that it happened, it was horrible, that sort of material just basically lying around in a place that had obviously been passed for us to stay. Without casting aspersions, I ask myself the questions: why? Were they his? Were they somebody else's that he had found? Was his mother aware that they were even there? And at 16 or 17, or any age, why would you show that sort of thing to a child; it just doesn't make sense.

For the rest of the trip I just didn't want to be there, we visited most of the sights of London, though again I don't really remember much, only the last one on the last day which was the Thames barrier. I distinctly remember as I brought a small model of its whist there, but never actually built it for some strange reason. I mean every kid wants to build models, well I did, but I didn't build this one for some strange reason. I also remember a poster of the Cutty Sark that I picked up and hung on my bedroom wall when I returned home. Why? I don't know, I just suppose I wanted it because they were giving them away, even back then if they were giving it for free I would be at the front of the queue even if I didn't want it...

Towards our last couple of months in primary school, the high school that I was going to was right across the road, big it was too. I can remember when I was sat in class looking out of the window thinking, 'shit' have I really got to go there. I mean everything was so nice in primary, one teacher, one room, you knew where you were, no interruptions, but going to high school was going to be so different.

I see it now from schools that I have worked in, the year seven , a lot of them struggle with that adaptation, moving around from class to class throughout the day, it must have an effect on their education to start, even towards the middle of year seven you can see some are still struggling, and all that the teachers say to them is "you should be grown up by now" or some shallow comment like that. Teachers these days don't seem to have the understanding, or they have lost the ability or even the will to be bothered for the students, it all seems to be about figures, stats and Ofsted. So many kids these days are getting left behind because of teachers and staff not giving a shit, I've seen and heard it in staff rooms and in school offices. The negative talk I heard at a school where I worked at for a while was shocking to the point where I refused to go into the staff room at all. I mean it wasn't even just gossip, it was purely smearing someone's character, it was bad, these are just kids, under 18. The stuff that was being spoken about was terrible. Admittedly kids are hard work sometimes and they do get a little bit cheeky, but to use and aim words and phrases like nutters and "he's special him", that's just damn right wrong. What really got to me was the fact that I was working with a few of these kids, so to hear things being said about them was just disrespectful and appalling, but it also made me want to work harder to get these kids what they needed.

It was the first week in September 1988, first day at high school, I recall the assembly hall, looking around at all of the other faces and heads that were sat down, what a daunting experience. But the worst was yet to come, the first class, I noticed straight away that I was the very different kid. I walked with a limp, wasn't quite fitting in, it was shit, I didn't want to be there, but I had no choice, it was the bottom set and from the word go no one wanted to do any writing or listening. They were like animals, every one of them fighting for themselves! Quickly you have to think how do I get on in the environment, the only way was to join in a hope that you're accepted, don't get me wrong, I'm not advocating that every kid should join in and cause complete havoc, but I felt that I was one on my own and would have died had I not have shown some sort of enthusiasm to be part of their club and in the end it didn't really cut any ice. Some work was achieved when certain individuals were off sick or removed from the class, the change was pretty instant as well, but they kept returning so the whole class would revert back to messing around as you do. Most of my time in high school was shit, I struggled anyway with listening and writing, I would lose concentration after 10 minutes as was noted in all my school reports all the time. Strange that in a way, they always noted it down, but never actually did anything about it, not a plan or something put in place to help, but they were quick enough to bring it up at parents evening. Even during PE lessons, I would just drift off right in the middle of the field in the dead of winter when it was freezing, just in a world of my own. Tennis in the summer, I clearly remember it being hot, and I would struggle to serve because it meant doing the two actions at once with my hands which for anyone that knows me is not happening; one hand goes one way, and the other wherever it feels like, so the teacher had a go at me in his deep welsh accent and told me to go and sit down for the rest of the lesson. I mean where was his encouragement? So there I was on the tennis court, sat on my arse, sun beating down with nothing to do. I lay back and just stared up into a deep blue sky wondering what I was doing here, watching the high altitude wafer thin clouds just drift by, at that point I was thinking that I could actually be anywhere in the whole world right now as all I could see was the sky. It was at that point that I also realised that I wanted to travel, I wanted to do something with my life, I was 14 years old. The following day because the maths teacher had pulled a sickie the head teacher took the lesson. Well, I say 'took' the lesson he just put the TV on and stuck a VHS in the video player. Now the head teacher was into riding bikes at the time. He used to turn up at school in the mornings with these figure hugging tight shorts on, it must have been a trend in the 90s for teachers to wear tight clothing for some reason as even the PE teacher wore the tightest of shorts that I have ever seen, anyway, this video was a stage of the Tour de France. Now at 14 years old the last thing you want to be watching in class with your mates is a load of fellas messing around on bikes in skimpy clothing, but unfortunately that was going to be the case this one Tuesday afternoon… I can tell you now that no one in the class was interested in the slightest. No one was ever going to become doctors or bankers from my class. They just weren't interested unless it involved kicking someone's head in, so there I was, back of the classroom, two choices, watch some French bloke with a pony tail ride around France with his mates on bikes, or scrape my name into the desk as like everyone else. I mean there were other distractions in the room like Tammy., She used to sit near the front of the class, a bit mouthy at times, , but I had a bit of a soft spot for her, but despite this on that day I sort of found myself hooked on the TV screen and watching this French fella riding up and down the Champs-Élysées being chased by and American. It was only a few years later that I realised the significance of that particular stage in the tour. Greg Lemond (USA) won the overall by just eight seconds from Laurent Fignon (FRA) on that very last stage! The entire race distance that year was 3285 km, so to take overall victory by such a small margin was pretty special. So there was I watching this race unfold, it was like no one else was in the classroom to which I suddenly became that absorbed and focused on the race that nothing else mattered. I went home that afternoon and fell in love with bikes, wanted to start riding and racing. That was the day that inspired me, the day that changed the direction of my life, though I didn't know it at the time, so I just carried on the daily grind in school. I didn't really have any aspirations to do anything. I remember they had a career woman come into school one afternoon, I was in year 10 I think, I met her in the library and we sat down, she had all these glossy magazines and stacks of books on the table in front on me. She said what is it that you would like to do, I swiftly replied with my elbows on the desk and my chin resting on my hands, "I would like to go home." No such luck unfortunately.

"Why don't we have a look," she said eagerly moving forward in her chair as if to want to take charge. I said I want to ride a bike in a softly muffled expression as the words drifted between my fingers, she gave me this almost evil ghastly look as if to say "OK what's next" as she sat there in her brown-coloured trouser suit. I'd like to meet her now though! OK so it didn't exactly work out straight away, but what does these days. I mean everything takes time to establish.

As the last few months passed by my GCSE exams were soon upon me, not really a thought I was relishing, but what student does. It must be worse these days because students have things drilled into them from such a young age about targets and results that need to be hit. The pressure must feel enormous, whereas back then no one really mentioned that side of things, you just did what you were taught and that was it. I can remember sitting most of my exams, well the ones that I had been entered for anyway, I remember sitting down with the paper in front of me thinking what is all this about, I really struggled with my English papers and probably should have had more time to complete them due to my slow processing that had been identified by the teachers over the years, but nothing had really been put in place for me. It was the same for most of the papers that I sat, my strongest was my geography where I scored A* with a merit and then there was my art which came out as A. My other subjects just flopped. I did what I could with the time that I had in the exams, but with the onset of fatigue and the fall in concentration levels the end result probably didn't show my full potential of what could have actually been achieved on them papers. OK! You could argue that I could have resat them, or even carried those on in college had I have gone, but to be honest I just wanted out of the whole thing and to just get on with life. So that was that. I remember the very last day in school, it was a full day so until 3.20 pm, the teachers had laid on some shitty performance that I can slightly recall. It was a look back at our time spent at the school which really was the last thing I wanted reminding of, but there you go; we sometimes have to do these little ritual happenings to please other people. The school had obviously done this for like probably ever so it was traditional, yeah. Me, I just wanted to get out. So 3.20 pm came and I remember walking out of the gates for the last time, I arrived home and no one was in, but there happened to be a half opened bottle of champagne in the fridge that obviously the parents had been guzzling the night before, I lifted it from the shelf and took a swig. My eyes watered instantly, and the bottle almost overflowed, but for me that was like a celebration,

I said to myself "Cheers" and could have very easily kept on drinking, but that would have left me in not a good position both physically and in the way of having to explain to the parents…

Chapter 5
The Apprentice

Learning the trade in my younger days at an early season time trial event.

With school done and dusted I had no intentions of going to college or university. With my time through education being what it had been, I couldn't have endured even more time trying to absorb the relentless sat at a desk with my head in books so therefore opted for the route of trying to self-fund my own path towards becoming a professional cyclist. I could finally visualise the road in front of me, it was to be a long one that I was prepared for, and a not so smooth at times, but for me I was going to be trying to achieve something that I had a passion for. It was the only thing that I wasn't bad at so the odds were more in my favour than the normal script of everything being stacked against me like they were in school…

So this plan that I had constructed, well! It was like looking at trying to get to the top of Everest wearing only a T-shirt, shorts and a pair of sliders... But hey, sometimes we have to set ourselves goals that are pretty much out of our reach in reality just to really push the envelope. Setting out to achieve the impossible can quite often install the drive that we need. Should those goals actually come to fruition then we can truly say that in our lifetime then we have achieved our dream. So here's the plan, I needed to have enough funds to live on and would enable me to support me through my sport which wasn't cheap at the time, but I couldn't let that deter me from my dream. Fortunately, I lived at home so I think I needed to find £30 a week rent, anymore would fund my racing and all the equipment I needed. I was looking at least 25 hours a week to train, 56 hours a week to sleep and another 40 working hours to give me around £100 a week at a very low minimum hourly rate back then of £2.50 for under 18 years of age, so that worked out at 141 hours a week, leaving me with 27 hours surplus... Well, take out at least seven hours eating time a week, another 10–12 hours travelling wherever, and then say six hours for any other commitments would probably leave me with about one hour of absolutely free time out of the 168 hours that we get a week thanks to the planet rotating at a constant velocity. *And kids of today reckon they have it bad...* So we now calculate that by around six to seven years of mind-bending commitment of beating your head against a brick wall day in day out with no guarantee of ever making it, fucking hard yeah, but you do it because of your inner drive, determination and absolute passion for success and not wanting to fail, because to live with failure would just screw you up completely. People go on about it all of the time; I see quotes on Twitter and Instagram about always living life to the full, never having regrets, to always chase your dream etc. It is right, but I think more of that kind of thing needs to be in schools now, not just the odd comment from a teacher or maybe a poster that's been shoved up on the wall to fill an unsightly gap. Kids need to understand that everyone has the ability to achieve whatever they want. Me, I did it a lot by myself because I was being told the opposite, being left out of PE lessons yet here I was trying to carve myself a future in sports as an athlete, my teacher would have had a right laugh for sure.

So the first 12 months I was finding it extremely difficult coming up against barrier after barrier, trying to find some sort of work that would give me the funds and the time that I needed to train and race. OK maybe I was being too ridged or setting the bar too high, but I couldn't really see any other way! You simply do it or you do not, that's your choice.

At the time there was a scheme called the YTS which was a youth training scheme that had been set up for school leavers. The pay was terrible, I think it worked out as 30 hours a week at £2.30 an hour, so about £70 a week, it was in a woodyard just sorting orders for customers, after a while it became a bit like slave labour as my duties would become more and more. The expectation wasn't high from the employer. At the end of the day you were just a school leaver in their eyes so they just took the piss. Well, if you think about it a company has a fresh out of school 16-year-old that is on a YTS programme where the company doesn't have to pay anything because it's the scheme that is paying the hourly rate, who isn't going to take advantage of that. I think I stuck it for six months and then found some other work not on the YTS, but in a shop as a stock replenishing technician! Sounds good. Don't it, don't be fooled, it was just a shelf filler, nothing glam though, these days you do get to wear a uniform with 'happy to help' written on the back... I mean seriously, do you really think they're happy to help. To them it's just a target on their back for customers to annoy them, there's no getting away from it, it follows them around like a bad smell, always on their shoulder. I even noticed the night staff wearing them in a superstore at 2 am not so long back. They're probably the worst ones to approach. One, they're working the graveyard shift for a reason, that most likely means they don't like customers, and two, if it were me, and someone at 2 am asked me where the gluten free rice cakes were I would most likely tell them to trot on...

The hours suited at this new job. The pay was OK so I was able to work on my training and the planning of my route to a professional career. It wasn't all smooth and adjustments needed to be made. I was also learning to drive which took a huge proportion of my income, but I needed to be mobile as that would give me the freedom to travel as well as being self-sufficient. Lucky lessons back then where only a tenner an hour plus if you block booked you got a discount. I must admit learning to drive took longer than I initially expected, but I think that was down to me not declaring my disability at the time as it just would have complicated things. So each time that I ran up the pavement or miss-judged a turning my right hand lost control on the steering wheel, or I accelerated away from junctions too quickly, nearly running in to the back of other cars as I lacked control in my right foot. The instructor just got arsey with me, then kept saying we needed more lessons. Really I just think he was being petty, it was a Nissan Micra with four gears, it was hardly the fastest 0–60 car on the roads at the time and he was controlling it more than me quite often with the dual control peddles which pissed me off so many times as the car would stop when I wasn't expecting it to, he would also keep pushing the clutch in like to the point where we were sat on the roundabout going absolutely nowhere with the accelerator fully open, revving its 1.1 engines bollocks out creating a holy show to passers-by. I am glad to say I eventually passed my test and I'm a much better driver... I think...

My riding was starting to come together by now. I was a few years into things, was gaining some good results and gaining confidence. I was still with the Chester road club, the cycling club that I had very first approached when I started. The guys there had been an absolute wealth of knowledge to get me started, but things where now starting to step up a level and I'd started to train with a good set of riders on weekends and on a Wednesday midweek. A couple of us used to meet on a Wednesday morning at the eureka café at the two mills on the Wirral, we'd go for around four hours, it used to push me on loads as these were some of the north wests up and coming talent at the time, the likes of Mark Baker and Steve Cummings, both representing Great Britain at junior level and for Steve he has gone on to win stages in the Tour de France, vuelta a espana and so on, and now rides for team dimension data. This was perfect training rides for me, you have to look when you're planning any programme at what is going to make you better, what are the areas that you need to and can access that are going to push you on to be that better athlete. On a couple of rides I would get dropped from the group, but you learn to stick at it because eventually your fitness and your skill will become better, chasing guys around whether in training or racing that are more advanced than you will in turn make you stronger.

Life is not always comfortable, let me explain a scenario; so it's 7 am and you look outside, it's raining or snowing, far from ideal, the majority of us would feel it reasonable to just get back in bed and snuggle under the covers, and see if it dries up later on in the day. I get it, it's relaxing, it's comfortable, but let me tell you that there is an undervalued benefit that comes from putting yourself in an uncomfortable situation, this is the exactly the situation to put on your training gear and head out into the day. You're not doing anything that's heroic or superhuman, You're doing it because it's different to your average person, it's doing something that most would view as irrational, but that's because you have that different mindset, that ability to put yourself in that undesirable situation that most people can't comprehend. You do it because you want it that little bit more, why is it you train in these conditions; the wet, the cold, it's because it's uncomfortable, you're out there on your own, going through it hour by hour while everyone else is in the warm, while everyone else is comfortable and there's value to that. It sucks to train in those conditions, but having that mentality, it doesn't leave you, when your showered and back in your warm dry clothes you then carry it into other parts of your life, your work, your school studies and just about anything you do from day to day for the rest of your life to meet your daily goals. You look at things differently, the key to success, find a way to get it done, so is it just a training session in undesirable conditions? You tell me…

In 1996, I suffered a blow to my progress during a race, it was a road time trial just on the outskirts of Chester on a Sunday morning, I was about halfway through when I was re-joining a very fast section along a dual carriageway, as I entered the bypass via the slip road I was descended off the roundabout when I ran into the back of a stationary car at around 46 kph. I vaguely remember anything apart from the paramedics in the back of the ambulance trying to get an intravenous drip into my right arm which wasn't happening because of my spasms in that side of my body from my previous head injury. I recall trying to say that it needed to go into the left arm, but I was completely out of it if I'm honest. Somehow, they must have heard because when I eventually did come around in hospital it was in fact in the left arm.

After a week in hospital I was discharged, I had made a complete mess of not just myself, but also totalled my bike and wrote off the back end of the car that I had hit. Healthwise I was told that I couldn't afford another bang to the head which obviously scared me a lot as I was now left thinking does that mean I can't race my bike in case of risk of crashing. All these thoughts where going around my mind, I was in no fit state to get back on my bike training so I just had to sit it out. Some weeks later I was eventually in some sort of condition to start back a low-level exercise. It was slow and quite frustrating at times; my face had taken the brunt of the accident. I had required stitches around my eyes, in my nose and lip. My eyes would not stop watering as they had become quite sensitive to air flow. I can remember going out on the bike for the first time and them just streaming to the point that I couldn't see anything; this went on for a few years after and even now one eye isn't completely right. During the rehab time I was dealt another blow after being issued with a ban from competition between March and September 1997 after it was deemed that the accident was purely my own fault and that I was riding without due care and attention, so that was my 97 season fucked before it had even started.

A whole season missed could have a huge impact on my progress both physically and mentally, but I couldn't do anything; that's the card that had been dealt, I had to take it. So I just rode my bike through the winter of 96/97, nothing really programme based. I spent the season with a focus on racing the last few road time trials of the season, then doing a few hill climbs in the October, it was something to aim at. I couldn't go a whole year doing no racing at all. I saved up and bought a replacement bike for the one that I had totalled, I was able to salvage a few bits from the wreckage of the other frame but not much.

The season of 98 drifted by, I had sort of lost a little bit of motivation and drive, I needed to change things over the next few years to relight my passion, I decided that I was going to join a new team that I knew had run trips into France to race from time to time, so that was the plan. I sourced a contact and my 1999 season was put into action. Things started really well with the new outfit; it gave me a sense of purpose. It was a young team with lots of aspirations. I was advised that to go and do some races in France at this stage may not be the right thing and to wait until the following year, I didn't mind being told that as it was good advice coming from a guy that I looked up to called Dave Baker, he was the father of Mark Baker who I used to train with occasional, so he was a great source of sound information. My results and fitness had come on a lot in 99 and as we rolled into 2000 it was to be a big year, we started with the Eddie Soens Memorial Race in March at Aintree race course; a race in the calendar that a lot of big name national riders and teams use to kick start their season. In some ways it's quite a beautiful race because of its history, not so much for the weather, that can sometimes hang over the event. This can range from sunny and dry spring-like conditions, to snow and ice or rain and wind, but whatever Mother Nature decides to greet you with on the day the riders still enjoy the battle.

With the season rolling by I got my chance to go into France for some racing. It was July time; we were taking the long drive south through the UK and into France via a ferry crossing. As we drove down towards Paris, I could feel the weather gathering the European style, with the temperatures becoming warmer the further south that we travelled. I recall having to stop a few times for water and refreshments. As we hit the outskirts of Paris I could sense the enormity of this beautiful city, it was rush hour traffic, we had all the windows down on the car as the wind rushed in hoping that it would cool us, but that was also very warm as it caught on your face when it whipped through the window and circulated the cabin, it was just nice to have a breeze on your face though.

We were staying in the suburb that was Gennevilliers in the north west area of Paris with a population of 41689, (that's just for those nerds among us), so this was to be our location for the long weekend. The hotel was pretty that we stayed in. If I stuck my head right out of the window, I could just see the Eiffel Tower at night all lit up which was really a bonus. We did a couple of training rides close by around the Longchamp horse racetrack, which was pretty special, we also did a few of the sightseeing monuments, but the focus was on the racing which would take place on the Sunday. It was an amazing feeling; my first time racing abroad and in France as well, the birth place of cycling and the Tour de France, the race I had watched in the classroom at school all them years ago, and now I was here. I had seen the Champs-Élysées in its full glory, the actual road that the race that I had watched had been won on.

The racing was very fast and furious, more than I had ever experienced in the UK, proper racing as I can remember thinking as we tanked along and cornered on tight cobbled roundabouts. There was no fantastic result for me, but the experience and feeling that weekend gave me was incredible. A big thanks to Dave and in fact the Baker family. It was Dave that ran the small team that I was part of that helped me not just with sound advice, but also equipment that he borrowed out to me to race on. It's people like Dave in not just the cycling and sporting world, but in just about anything really, those unsung heroes that give their time to help others achieve.

I returned to the UK where I finished out the season on the road and was then invited to a British cycling national track championship to be introduced to the Paracycling world. I was asked if I would be interested in taking part in some testing and some track sessions to see if I could meet the criteria to be part of the team going forward starting in 2001. Of course, I took this opportunity straightaway without hesitation. It was December time 2000, I was part of a coach lead world class performance programme session, I met with a guy called Marshall Thomas who was one of the GB coaches at the time, he had also sorted me a bike that I could use as I had never ridden the track before, nor did I have a track bike so the whole experience was completely new. A track bike has no brakes and no gears, it is a fixed wheel so you can't stop peddling like on a conventional road bike. I shit myself when I first cocked on this thing, it was so alien to me that I hated it, but this was my opportunity, so I had to go with it.

Having half mastered this thing I was on, I now had to go on to the track, again I had never ridden it. *Fuck*, I can remember thinking as I climbed myself up onto the boards of the Manchester velodrome. I had to ride fast for fear of falling off in the banking that are at a 45-degree angle, but the rush I was receiving was something that I hadn't experienced before. Was it because I was on the track or was it because of the moment, I had to be careful not to get to wrapped up in the situation. I needed to stay focused on why I was here. I was asked to do some timed laps, then later on I was introduced to another coach who said that they were very interested, and would I be available from January to take on a structured programme going forward to the European championships in the September of the following year. This took me by surprise, but of course I said yes. I had achieved a huge mile stone that I had been working towards for the past 6 years, I was on the edge of a full-time professional career doing something that I had fallen in love with as a teenager at a time when I didn't really have any sort of direction in my life, and should the following season work out. I had no doubt in my mind as I now had the input from some world class coaching and facilities.

So after all the formalities the 2001 rolled in, Marshall Thomas was to be the coach who would be overseeing my programme that would see me progress forward; it was like nothing that I had done before, the testing alone was just another level, then there was my nutrition side of things, the physiotherapy that I was introduced to, it would all make a difference, a whole new injection of ideas that would change me from the amateur cyclists that I was into the champion that I am today. There was more detail placed on training rather than racing, with us just targeting a few events at certain times of the year to fit into specific training goals and structures. The main focus for the year was obviously September at the European championships. I spent a lot of time based down in Alsager on the university campus as that is where the GB team had accommodation set up for riders that were road and track-based, so I would spend a few days away from home at a time when we had a block of track work or road training to do as it was easier to access what I needed in order to build on my training and improve my performance lifestyle.

This was a massive shift for me, my whole life had changed, I was now on a path for success, buying into everything that was offered to me.

After some great results at the national track championships in August of 2001 in Manchester, I was selected for the team that would travel to Switzerland just a few weeks later for the European championships.

Chapter 6
So the Deeper Me

I was always a bit of a loner, always drifted off, if I was asked to describe myself in a few words, "I would probably have to ask which Rik would you like me to describe, you see there are two Riks, there's Rik the cyclist and athlete, and then the real Rik, the softly quiet-mannered human being. I think most people who know me or are quite close to me would agree that I can be a bit of a twat in the respect of the athlete side of me, that's when I have my head on to do something. I'm selfish, I scatter things out of the way, ignore everyone and anything that is going on regardless of whether it be a family gathering or someone suffering illness. Natalie, who I was with for a huge part of my cycling career, would probably be the best to ask (or not), I don't deal with other people being ill at the best of times. I tend to not become too engrossed in it. A lot of people view me as not caring whenever situations like that happened, and that may well be why when it has come to relationships, things just become a little disrupted. The thing is, I do care, and can see that I'm being selfish, but that's how I am, I become that focused on say a target, that I wouldn't, and probably still would not, make any allowances to deter me from trying to achieve whatever I had set out to do. In the week that followed my wedding there was a track competition being held in Germany that I had been selected to go to, so literally 48 hours after the wedding I was back on the track in Manchester training, then off on to a plane to Düsseldorf instead of taking off for a honeymoon to some exotic location. It was this point that I started to see that I was struggling to separate the two parts of my life. For years there had only been the one focus, one thing to think about.

Looking back now, since I left school, possibly even further back than that, anxiety was a big thing in my life. Although I didn't really recognise it as stress, it was more the understanding really. I have maybe gone around with my eyes closed about these sorts of things, just got on with doing, but if I scrutinised it, I was possibly suffering from depression from a teenager. It wasn't in the press so much back then like it is now about teenagers with mental health issues, there wasn't the exposure to political news; well, obviously it was on the television, but as a kid, a young teenager I was just out a lot, causing mischief or having fun. Once I left school the rigors of life were put upon me. I did find it difficult to get on, to fit in, and I suppose I used riding a bike a mechanism to sort of escape from them kind of anxious feelings that I was having. I lost myself in riding, training, and anything else to do with bikes as I established a comfort zone or safety netting from the clutter that I would call normal life. I wasn't mollycoddled by my parents, nor did they treat me any different from my brother. If I'm completely honest I still don't feel that I have developed, I let the child in me come out far too often. I still have those same feelings that I had when I was at school, and still carry on the same processes that I did back then which I find a little frustrating at times, and getting married didn't change that at all, so when I went to this competition instead of on a honeymoon right after the wedding it didn't really bother me. I just carried on like normal. I have questioned it time and time again, but don't really seem to get anywhere with it.

For almost two and a half years after my marriage broke up I kept myself to myself, my feelings tight close to me as I was not wanting to ever be hurt and feel the same feelings of dejection and absolute worthlessness. I would refuse to go out to meet new people, refuse to engage with anybody else unless it was through my work which was purely professional so there was no need to develop that into anything other than work. I distanced myself from family, and the so-called circle of friends that were around when Natalie and I were together. My verdict of these so-called friends just a few weeks into the breakup gave me much to mull over, what did they think of the break up? Were they blaming me? What were my feelings towards them? Why hadn't anyone called me? Were they talking about me in a bad way? This was one of them occasions where I started to self-doubt myself, in fact after some time thinking about things it brought me to the decision that they were actually quite a shallow bunch of people. Not one of them ever made contact to ask how I was doing, or if things were OK, but I already knew that they were of this sort of character when we used to go out back then, very materialistic and self-centred. I never really took to them from the word go and would just go along with things that were organised by them or by Natalie because it would keep everyone else happy and save any confrontation.

I have never been one to burn up the social scene, or one for social gatherings. Even with family, I would always try and avoid them situations at every cost as I just didn't feel comfortable in that environment. Obviously, it has never gone unnoticed or unquestioned, even from myself. I tried to self-analyse, always asking myself why was I like this for years in everything I have ever done. Was I suppressing myself for some reason, was it something that had been there from a young age, part of my make up or was there something missing from my life that I hadn't yet found? This was a time of very mixed emotions. I was still feeling much pain and anger from the breakup and turmoil that something on that scale deals you. I couldn't stand the thought of any more upset, I wanted to feel that I was in control, well as much as I could be, it was big serious stuff that perhaps you only sit down to address properly maybe once or twice in a life time, and this was one of those occasions. Had I for all these years been doing things because it seems it's the right thing to do, or because I had thought that it is what you are meant to do because everyone else is doing it or because I have been programmed and had it installed in me that it's how life goes.

I was the Astronaut that I always wanted to be stood there behind my friends Steven and Philip.

As I sit here now sipping coffee in a Starbucks nestled inside a motorway services, having just observed the 11 o'clock 2 minutes silence witnessing everyone else going about their Sunday business, it's just dawned on me that no one actually gives a fuck about anyone. I was watching people coming and going, all absorbed in their own little worlds, but with that and everything in life there is a flip side; there are also people stood in churches, may be at other gathering locations around the world going about their business because they believe it's the thing to do, the same pattern that they have grown up with, and that everybody else does the same thing. I am not disrespectful, nor saying it is the wrong thing to do either way, but I'm merely pointing out that how confused that I have been for a lot of my life, is it the way in which my brain processes situations that I have found myself in all of this time that has led me to being so unsure about what to actually do with my time other than ride a bike.

For me I want to be seen for who I am now and not what has happened to me in the past. If I'm completely honest with you I don't want to be judged at all, but unfortunately that's people's first instinct, but it was that accident back in 82 that has shaped my life into the person that I am today. Yeah, I have my faults, but don't we all. I'm selfish, I can be a right twat at times, I know that, but to be determined and achieve things that you have a passion for, may it be in your line of work or just your life in general you have to realise that if you want something bad enough then you have to make sacrifices, whether that be long term or short term and sometimes you do end up pushing situations or even people out of the way in order to achieve what you've set out to do. I know I did that; I didn't do it intentionally, it was just and still is part of my makeup, we are all different. I know my pitfalls, my characteristics which to anyone looking in would think I've got it so wrong, but unfortunately that is my drive, it's what has got me through tough times, through times where you think that it is impossible as all the odds are stacked, everyone is against you and there looks to be no way out. But then, by channelling every ounce of belief, every spare drop of energy that you have no matter what else is going on, then that's the one thing that is going to get you to where you want to be. That may take a minute, it may take an hour, but when you get there, the reward is worth all the hurt and anguish that you may have gone through over the past days, weeks, months or even years. But not only that, it teaches you a valuable lesson that no text book can offer you, it's the confidence to know that anything that you come up against in the future is just another hurdle to get over, just another process to go through to get you to where you want to be.

So the deeper me, the fascinating side of which many people don't get to see, the side that probably my mother and father don't even have a clue that exist, from a young age I have been a dreamer. We all have dreams and places of comfort, going through primary school its where my daydreaming first started. I suppose I used it as a possible escape or get away from maybe my school work or as a blanket for certain occasions that may have or not have happened during the school day, I would end up in trouble on so many occasions from just starring out of the window during our lessons, but it gave the sense of a much better place, I have never spoken about these day dreams before and now I'm actually writing this down it brings a smile to my face and I can now see how those thoughts developed as I got a bit older into the things that I like for real in my life; the warmth of a real fire, or the fresh air that surrounds mountains, I love a good open fire, you can't beat the crackling sound of wood or the smell of soot from coal. We actually had a real fire in one of our houses which was such a delight to come home to in the winter. I also used to love adventure as a child, a friend around the corner and I used to throw on our camouflage clothing, smear wet mud on our faces and head off into the woods. I used to love being out in the fresh air; getting muddy, cold and wet was all part of growing up which I suppose when I'm out now training in similar conditions it doesn't faze me so much because it's what I used to having fun all those years back, in a way it has built up a resilience because of the association.

I have tried hard over my life not to let everyday stresses cloud my inner character, maybe turn me into something that I am not, but I feel that they have had a huge bearing on a lot of my qualities. I'm a very private individual, I don't like noise or bright lights, my biggest fear in life is what other people may think of me. it's a fear that you can have that if not addressed can become quite a black cloud over you as all of its reactions and battles taking place inside of you, like it's your own private nuclear war that starts with a burn deep in your core to then erupt, but somehow still be contained within the boundaries of your own body. You then privately deal with the aftermath and not to let anyone suspect that you're having issues. I guess that is why I keep myself to myself. I'm in a sense controlling the battle and keeping my biggest fear under control, or as much as I can, I would really love not to have this quality that holds me to its demands, but I have been unable to rid it of my system.

I sleep on a futon bed; I have trouble staying in a normal bed and therefore feel safer closer to the ground should I fall out at any time. I used to think at the time when I was married that the wife was pushing me out of bed each time that I would wake up in the mid-air section between the mattress and the floor, gasping for life in an almost dreamlike effect before swiftly hitting the floor, but no. On training camps I would regularly fall from the bed in whatever hotel we were in, I've often startled my team GB cycling mates Darren Kenny or Jody Cundy in the dead of night with a yell or an impromptu swear word as I woke en route to the floor. I don't know if it's problem, a phobia or just the fact that I have no spatial awareness once my head assumes the horizontal position on the pillow, so to limit any major damage to myself it serves to sleep low. I have a sweet tooth for sugared cola bottles, I could live on them and nothing else if left. My favourite chocolate is Cadbury's buttons, again I could just eat packet after packet until I exploded like a molten of larvae spewing from a volcano. At every opportunity I have to drag myself away from the sweet aisle whenever I'm in a shop for fear that I will give in to my inner desires to just ravish myself with chocolate buttons. I don't drink carbonated drinks, but my favourite every time is Pepsi, always has been. For me when you drink it, the fizzy particles seem smaller to all the other fizzy drinks, a bit like Aero chocolate bar is to Cadburys Whisper bars, you sensing it now, yeah? You know I'm right, or just too analytical.

Old fashioned sweet shops are the rage in towns now, they are like the devil standing on the street corner for me, luring me over to that side of the road hoping that I will drop to my knees in shear desperation.

I've always liked drawing. I was good at it at in school age, it is something that I started to bring into my school mentoring sessions with students that I worked alongside. I would use it in a therapy type of exercise, and at the end of my time with whoever I was working with, I would draw them a picture of whatever they chose. A lot of drawings that I produced when I was younger were based around scenery from my daydreaming, I did hundreds of doodles of mountains and sun sets, absolute bonkers. Should have done one for my GCSE work instead of a bowl of fruit, I may have achieved a merit then on my final mark.

According to my mother I used to follow my dad around like a shadow when I was really young, would never leave his side, whether that be in the garden or the house. I used to copy things that he did, but I think that would be the norm given any father and son relationship. Someone you look up to, someone you just want to be like, that was the case, even going to work with him from around the age of three, traveling the country with my teddy bear to hand to keep me company.

It's all a bit sketchy anything that I remember before my accident, it's as if my memory has been wiped clear on anything that happened pre-1982. I was, and still am, a relatively easy going person, some people have even said that if I was any more laid back then I would be horizontal, but I just think they may be getting confused slightly, assuming that I'm portraying the take it easy approach when really I'm just saying "I don't know what you're on about, I'm just humouring you..." but even then they would probably think that I was just playing with them.

I haven't any intolerances to anything like a lot of people have today, I have never understood that one. I can't recall any such things when I was younger, we had one kid in the whole school with an inhaler that everyone wanted a puff on, as it was seen as the new futuristic tool that gained you super powers after just one puff, so I remember as we all huddled at break time in the boys toilets, leaving someone as look out by the door, if only we knew back then what we know now about the inhaler, wow I can feel the difference it made even now... And as for reactions to food, well that just didn't exist, not like these day, I mean some people can't stand near cheese without their lips bubbling up, or having a panic attack at even the thought of it, yesteryears standards have slipped somewhat, and society has become soft as shit.

Another love and passion of mine is space, as in the universe, I can gaze for hours on clear nights, just a wonder of endless time above our heads. It's one place that I would give just about anything for, to travel to the international space station and spend some time just looking back at the rock that we live on. I watched Felix Baumgartner take his space jump in 2012, and I have to admit, I was slightly jealous. I mean who wouldn't want to drop from the edges of our planet, just the adrenalin rush alone would be enough to keep me happy for the rest of my life! Counting out the view, and everything that a feat like that would stand for, I would also love to go to the moon one day, but somehow, I'm not sure that will happen either. My fascination with the stars and space started after watching Superman as a little boy on the TV, seeing him fly around the earth, and then watching Superman 2 with the opening few scenes being that of the moon! At roughly the same time I received some space themed Lego which just heightened my vivid young imagination about wanting to go into space. Even at my friend's birthday party I was so thrilled as he had an astronaut play outfit with the helmet, the boots, the whole shebang! I can remember trying to contain my excitement as I climbed into it, squeezed my feet into the boots, then pulled on the helmet. The tingle I was feeling was out of this world as I stood there hearing nothing except my breathing cocooned inside of the helmet. Oh, the joy and jubilation were, and still is, unforgettable, I was on the moon that day stood there in that suit.

I sometimes dream that maybe after we die then our soul has the ability to travel through time, and see all the universe in its full glory, because that's what it is. I suppose out there in space is time, it's where it all happens, the creation of what we are today, and what we can and will become. I'm no philosopher by any stretch of the imagination, but it's hard to deny that it probably is the main denominator in what we are.

I've spent many hours lying in bed thinking about this kind of stuff: why are we here in the first place? I mean where are we in the grand scheme of things? I'm in no way religious or follow any sort of faith, just your average atheist. So what about space? Is it really endless? I mean, if you were to take a spaceship and fly out, do you just keep flying and flying, could you just fly forever, how could space just go on forever, and if it doesn't, what's at the end? And to go the other way: what was at the beginning of time? What was before time? Nothing? But what is nothing? How could there be nothing?

So we are here, a living organism on a piece of rock that is suspended in a cloud of partials made up of around 250 billion stars that make up a two armed spiral galaxy we call the Milky Way, and with that it becomes really interesting. So there could be as many as two trillion galaxies in the universe, each of these galaxies can contain anywhere from 200 billion to one trillion stars, so now if you multiply the number of stars in our own Milky Way galaxy by the estimated number of galaxies in the observable universe, you get around 1 septillion stars, yeah it's a word! Septillion, it's like the number 1 followed by twenty-four zeros, our brains aren't really capable of comprehending numbers this large by just reading them, so just say for instance we were to name every star in the Milky Way galaxy, then say we can name one star per second, at that rate alone it would take just shy of 8000 years to name them all, this serves as a humbling reminder of the tininess of us, and the enormity of the universe, and just maybe, we are the only living thing…

Other things I like are retro things, I have some original items from when I was younger which I'm hoping that in years to come I can go appear on Dickenson's real deal or some old junk show where you queue for hours on end, to then be told that what you have isn't of value, about my luck, but we live in hope! I was never a big movie watcher, but over the last few months I have to admit that I have watched an awful lot of this Netflix, I spent one whole day just sat watching film after film not having to move if I didn't need to, when it was mentioned to me before I couldn't see the attraction, but having had a lot of time on my hands lately, and with the advent of my eating habits going to the wall a bit, it definitely made some days more bearable for sure.

Since September last year I have been living in a mews type apartment block, it's a small setting with around 12 apartments, it's fairly quiet. I never really see anyone throughout the day, and with the added bonus of a funeral director to the rear of the block, its dead quite at night as well.

The start line for the 3km pursuit of my first international competition for
Great Britain at the 2001 European championships in Switzerland.

It's kind of hard living on your own, it took a bit of an adjustment, this whole
period since the marriage broke up had been the first time I have ever lived alone.
It has its good bits I suppose, like coming and going, not being answerable to
anyone, being able to find the TV remote when you want it, but they're the little
insignificant parts to living alone I say. Quite often I feel a shadow of my former
self, I used to do a lot around the house when I was with Natalie; cleaning,
cooking, tidying up, and that sort of stuff, nothing to really shout about, not
because she was a messy person or she didn't want to do them things, but they
were things that I enjoyed doing while Natalie was working, like a house husband
as to say. It would give me massive pleasure in knowing that she would return
to a tidy house and a cooked meal each night. I suppose that was a part of my
love for her, to look after her, so yeah it now seems like I have an empty part of
my life that I have failed to fill at the moment. I feel in a bit of a rut and that
nothing exciting will happen again. OK so house cleaning isn't something to get
singing and dancing about, but I was as busy as an ant farm, feeling the thrill of
the splendid mechanics that Mr Dyson himself spent years designing, no really!
It was more the fact that why I was doing it that made the so-called chores easier,
so yeah with now living on my own the chores tend to take a back seat now as I

don't get the same satisfaction from doing them in a sense. Saying all that though, I have never really felt or classed anywhere as home. For many years during my sporting years I was effectively living out of a suitcase a lot of the time so never really settled anywhere. Although we had a house, or rather places that we lived they never felt like home, I found it easier staying in hotels and the like. I still feel like that now, the simple life, yeah.

I'm a massive believer in giving back. I find myself now in a position to be able to do that after my sporting career and back in 2011 I became a patron to Claire House Children's Hospice that helps seriously and terminally ill children live life to the full. They also provide support for their families, it's an amazing charity with the work that it carries out, but you wish that there wasn't a need for such charities. Kids make the world a happy place without even trying, it's heart breaking that lives are cut short due to illnesses and the like, but with the help from such charities it's about making the best of the time that some children may have.

Chapter 7
A Decade on Two Wheels

Sitting on the start line of any event can be quite a daunting feeling, for years I would rock up at the local club event on a Thursday night, hoping to better the time you posted the week before, but now things were about to step up to another level. It was early September 2001, as the plane's wheels touched the Tarmac at Zurich International Airport I can remember gazing out of the window thinking, *The hills that I can't see are definitely not filled with the sound of music*, I was not impressed on my first impression of Switzerland, it was cloudy, and pissing it down like you would not believe. Typical, I should have guessed, and not really expected much else, or maybe I had been exposed to too many films and pictures in books as a child where Switzerland had been portrayed as a green, fresh-aired, non-polluted fairy tale land where the dark clouds of despair and misery were held back by the freshly laid snow-capped mountains that I was used to seeing on a Sunday afternoon as I watched ski Sunday on BBC 2 in my younger days. This was by far not the case as we proceeded via coach through the hustle and bustle ridden streets of Zurich en route to the industrial-sized hotel. Was this it? Was Julie Andrews and her wonderful mountain scenes all just a stage in the back streets of London that was pinewood studios. Surely not, surely that beautiful land must exist somewhere amongst the gloom, but no, it wasn't to be on this, my first international trip as a Great Britain professional rider, even on first arrival at the velodrome I could see that it was made up of World War Two type concrete and not some beautiful laid pine construction like in Manchester that ran just as smooth as the Swiss rail system.

Not to let my disappointment of my first impression of Switzerland dampen the reason why I was really here, it was straight on with the procedure of building bikes, and then a recon of the road courses followed by a few training sessions at the velodrome to get the feel of the grey dull concrete slabs that made up the 300 metres of track to be raced on. Yes that's 300 metres so not even the Olympic standard layout of a 250m. So the two events that I was to ride, the pursuit and the kilo had different calculations on the number of laps that I was used to doing before I left the UK. Oh and did I forget to mention it was an outdoor track, so even the weather was to be thrown in as a factor, not that I let little details like that warp my competitive mind, I was here to race for the first time with a GB jersey on my back, so even snow itself was not going to stop play in my mind.

The feeling of trepidation filled my first few days, it was so far from the club events that I had been so used to taking part in. The club standard rock up, pay your subs and spend anything between 20 minutes and an hour throwing your life down on the pot hole ridden roads and dual carriageways, hoping to overhaul the stopwatch of a 70-year-old veteran of the sport who had earned the privilege of time keeper, and who would be sat week in week out in a deck chair at the start and finish line, all eagle-eyed counting the riders as he ticked them off his clipboard and marked down their time as they finished. You carry all the excitement that you have now made it to the level that you always dreamt about, that you could only think about during your training rides as a novice, with the added pressure now that you feel because you are at such a huge point that anything less than winning would be a fail. We had a few days training to occupy my mind and my then roommate Barney Storey would keep me entertained during the long hours spent doing not a lot but relaxing. This was another component that was new, rooming with someone, a stranger really, roommates are characters that you need to be able to get on with. I mean no one wants to be stuck with someone that drives you mad, snores or can't stop chatting…fortunately Barney is one of those guys that would bring peace to a war-torn country if he was deployed.

So once I had gone through the formalities of classification and the rituals of that particular process it was down to racing. My first even up was the 1-km TT, the lap calculation was three laps and a bit as opposed to the normal four laps, it's quite a disadvantage doing the kilo on a 300m track because the event is all about speed and power, so with less corners because of the track geometry you don't benefit from the sling shot effect of the bankings in the corners as much. Nevertheless, I had a job to do. It was a cold day and I remember wearing leg warmers. The gun went off and the next I remember was crossing the finish line a little confused as I had lost count of laps and which side of the track that I was actually on. I think my actual time was 1.13.8 which was good enough to secure me my first European gold medal. This was just what I needed, the feeling to steady my nerves and relieve my thought process and approach to the rest of the event. The following day was to be the 3km pursuit, but as we arrived back at the hotel something terrible had happened, the date was in fact September 11th 2001. The hotel was crowded with people all gathered around the televisions in the hotel reception, I could not take it all in and we made our way up to our room where we switched the TV on. It was all unfolding live as we watched, one of the towers had been hit at this point, I recall standing there in my boxer pants as the other tower was hit by a plane, I just stood there and looked at my teammate Barney Storey who was lay on his bed, we didn't say anything, just looked at each other, almost communicating telepathically as to what we had just seen. For hours after we watched the whole situation unfold on this tiny TV screen, absolutely horrendous. I don't remember the rest of the evening nor the next morning or even my race that following day. That catastrophic moment placed everything into context of how insignificant we actually are, it made me realise that I needed to embrace this moment in time and not become too tied up in what other people were doing performance wise, as I say the race that followed that evening was really just a blur. I came away with a gold medal, but that's all I can remember. The situation and meaning of being there had changed, when people use the saying, "Do you remember where you were on such and such a day", like a lot of people will remember the moon landing and where they were, well, this is one of them moments for myself like thousands of people worldwide as to the magnitude of this one event.

My debut international race and my first major title at the European Championships in Zurich Switzerland 2001.

So straight after the track competition was over, we travelled on to the road events a few days later, but things just didn't feel right with what was going on in the world. The constant talk being about the news and media was the subject that filled the majority of the days. A few more days later and it was the road time trial, this was an event that I had been looking forward to since the start of the trip as it's a discipline that I hold a lot of passion for. After the events of the past couple of days I needed to get myself focused in order to produce the ride of the year by winning the event. We had the chance to do a recon of the course on several occasions before race day, it was a cracking little course, flat with a few twisty bits to spice things up at pace. During the warmup I misjudged a corner that I was navigating and ended up kissing the Tarmac. this shocked me a little as I could sense that I was becoming maybe a little over enthusiastic to get going, I took a couple of minutes to gather myself before proceeding to the start ramp. As I left the start-house, I felt on top of things and produced an absolute storming ride to win by over a minute from my closest rival. For me that one event was why I was here. It's the one that I wanted to win above everything else, so we rolled on to the formalities of the road race where I finished within the bunch which was to be expected. So that was it, my first major championships in Great Britain colours, of course I was made up with my performances and achievements but I will never forget the global tragedy that hit every human on the planet in one way or another on that day, and for years later. It was all a bit of a whirlwind, something was actually working out for me, I felt great, I felt I had a purpose and a reason to look at life slightly different.

So after a few weeks of relaxing time off the bike and having signed a contract as a professional cyclists on the GB cycling team it was straight into training and planning for 2002 and the world championships that were to be held in Germany in August. With a new coach and a full programme of staff working in all areas of the sport that I could access for support, all I had to do was think about riding my bike, something that I had loved from as young child. My training went from 25 hours a week to 30 hours, five extra hours a week doesn't sound a lot, but it really stretched me. It gave me that little bit more I needed to develop myself both physically and mentally. I recall being absolutely shattered at the end of each week, and the months that were through the winter really tested me beyond belief, but I had this bigger picture in sight. We were two years out from the Paralympic Games that were going to take place in Athens, Greece in 2004 so all that I was doing now was aimed at preparing myself for that event. The mental side of things would be paramount to this, dealing with the pressures of a huge event and having to produce the performance of a life time needs foundation, you can't just rock up, never having prepared and expect miracles, it all starts somewhere, and that somewhere was here. Yes, I had gotten myself to this point on what I knew and the training that I had done in the past, but this was a new level that required expert input and practices that I had never done or heard of before, but now I had access to world class funding and some of the country's top coaches at the time it was all to be absorbed.

2002 was a full programme of training camps and races that had been all planned out for me, so it was a case of keeping healthy and sticking to the script.

Whatever I do in training I like it to be proven before I sign myself to doing any such programme, so a lot of the training that I had done in the past up to this point was sessions and plans that I had researched via the Internet or from watching documentaries on television that other athletes had done. With the whole world class performance programmes that had been born through the national lottery funding scheme, things were still within its early stages of growth. the GB cycling team had just two years earlier came away from the Sydney 2000 Olympic Games with a gold medal from the likes of Jason Queally, and the lottery funding was a huge part of the success of British athletes now right across a range of sports.

For myself I was now part of this and I needed to take every opportunity that was presented to me either competing wise or coaching because it was the catalyst that would make me a better person, as an athlete and a human being.

2002 was more a learning curve, I failed to achieve much on the world stage having a disastrous world championship due to illness during the event. I had matured as an athlete through 2002 which was to carry me forward for many years after. 2003 again was filled with disappointment at international level again. I don't know what was wrong, I just wasn't able to string anything together, this in turn brought on my anxieties and I started to question myself, what was I doing wrong? Was I just not up to holding an elite level? Was I not fuelling myself in the right way? All these thoughts start to impact negatively on you which then brings in the demons. In spite of my development that I thought was going on, this was now the first point in my professional career that the cracks were starting to show and the low self-esteem that I used to suffer with at school was now starting to creep into this part of my life. So 2004 came and I was feeling confident as to my levels of fitness and focus to carry forward towards the qualification period for the Paralympic Games in the September, but yet another injection of disappointment was to land at my feet. In April, I was diagnosed with glandular fever which knocked me mentally as well as physically; nevertheless I ran myself through all the pre Paralympic selection processes of testing and all the protocols, but unfortunately I missed out in gaining a place on the team. I shut myself away, I didn't really want to talk to anyone and found it hard to face people when the conversation would pop up as to how I was getting on. I felt ashamed, and some days were unbearable to deal with. I had spent the past three years dealing with firstly becoming this full-time athlete that from my first international appearance I was instantly thrust to the top spot on the podium, to then spend the following two seasons going backwards and struggling to understand why the situation had spun in the opposite direction to now missing out on Paralympic selection and having to deal with the news that I had a virus that would take a while to clear my system. What came next was the nail in the coffin. Shortly after I was to break my ankle in a pretty bad way which left me needing my leg to be pinned and plated and having to wear a foot fracture brace for eight weeks, I clearly remember whilst lying in that hospital bed feeling very bored, frustrated and in yet another dark place in my life, that I needed something to focus on, all this shit that I'd been dealt, but I had to keep fighting no matter how hard it was. I looked at the national racing calendar, and could see that the national para-cycling time trial championship were in around four weeks' time, so there was me, lay in this bed with my leg supported in the air because of the swelling, thinking, *Can I race in 28 days' time?* Pure madness but I needed a fix and quick. I spent the next five days in the same position before they discharged me, two days after arriving home I was on the turbo trainer turning my legs, that was just seven days after the operation, to say that it was uncomfortable would be an understatement, but I had set myself a goal, and that's what I was going to do, as the weeks went by I was getting back to some sort of fitness that I was happy with, so I was still having to wear the foot brace and each time I went back to the hospital they would adjust it to allow me some more movement, each time they would ask how I was doing and if I was taking things easy and not rushing the healing process, I would just nod my head, I didn't really want to tell them that I was in full training mode and racing a national event in less than two weeks. I felt that they may put some sort of block on me competing and that's not what I wanted. So in the final few days before the race, which was down in the Leicestershire area, I had arranged for a friend to drive me there and do all of the setting up of bike etc. He would collect me at 4am to start the journey which was the most uncomfortable journey. My ankle had decided over night that it was going to swell a little so all the way there my foot was elevated up on the dashboard. We stopped a few times because at some points it was unbearable and I needed to just get out and move around. I remember at one point him saying to me whether I thought it was a good idea. I replied by saying, "No, but we are nearly there so let's keep going."

Once we arrived, I got my head in the zone which in turn allowed me to forget about the ankle, *well*, as much as I could do.

I arrived at the start line after my warmup with other riders asking what I was doing there. I sort of shrugged my shoulders and answered by saying, I thought I would come and make up the numbers. The race was a complete blur. I recall two stretches of road that I was on, one where I was sitting turning the biggest gear I had on the bike, and the other section was an uphill drag where I would normally be out of the saddle, but on this occasion I was limited to what I could do. I can recall crossing the finish line and decking it on a grassy verge after the effort I had put in over the last 3 km. The outcome was I won that event by just two seconds from the next guy, I was national champion! The drive home I must say was horrendously uncomfortable, but with a national jersey in hand I was pretty chuffed!

It took my ankle a little longer to recover, but that was me for the rest of the year. I had achieved something, not exactly what I wanted, but it was more the long-term mental positivity that it installed in me to say that whatever is presented to you no matter how devastating it may seem at the time you can always pull through, you just need to keep setting yourself targets and take steps to achieve them, no obstacle is too tall nor impossible to conquer.

So rolling into a new Olympic cycle, four years of planning and prepping for the next games that were to be taking place in Beijing in 2008, we had a big year in 2005. A few new members of back room staff would bring new venture to the team. Dave Mellor became the new manager, a guy with such a great vision for the team long term, a logical thinker and a great mentor that I took to. In any field of sport or the working environment it's always good to have a mentor, someone to look to for sound information, someone to talk to about any issues that you may have, a reliable source that you value and can have in your tool box for when time may become difficult. We did lots of traveling with a world championship taking place in the USA in July and a European championship in Holland in September, not to mention the standard national events held for both road and track disciplines. This year I was looking for some big international results to start to rebuild my way after the previous three sessions being somewhere stagnant. We smashed through the start of the year using a lot of racing in a conditioning type of training effect to arrive at the end of June in good shape for the cerebral palsy world championships which were over in the USA in New York State. Again this trip was remembered for other reasons as well so there was just the three riders that would fly out to the states with I think it was three members of staff, so myself, roommate Darren Kenny, and David Stone, staff were Dave Mellor team manager; Marshall Thomas, coach and Pete Taylor, (Spike) the mechanic. This was to be a real close knit trip, with so few personnel and being away for two weeks you have to be able to get on with people and the mixture we had here was just right, both professionally and personally. So the first day we arrived it was late afternoon and I recall once we had cleared the airport and arrived at the hotel. My first recollection was that we were sat on a low fencing at the side of a highway close to our hotel figuring out where we were going to eat that evening. We were all a bit jet lagged so I don't think many of us were bothered, just as long as we got some food. By this time Spike had collected the hire vehicle and off we went, just down the road there was a small place we pulled up at and proceeded into, the feel of this place was just like something that you would see in a mafia film, and I wasn't the only one to notice that fact, even Darren commented as we were shown to our seats by these three huge Italian American guys in black suits, that he felt uneasy about eating here. I mean Darren, he comes from a small village that sits in the new forest, so for him this must have been exactly that of a movie scene, but I think in the end we were all so tired that it got to the point that we just didn't care as long as we got food.

So the morning after, and having had a lay in, we were off to the local outdoor track where we would be competing in a few days' time. It was a 400-metre Tarmac Track with a huge bump coming out of the last turn from years of weathering, we had a couple of training sessions before the competition started, whilst there we got chatting to a few of the locals, and it was mentioned that the week before we arrived that there was a shooting there. I remember Darren's description of the whole procedure was quite an in-depth analysis of how a guy had been chased by the cops, bolted the fence on to the track, but was then shot. *Welcome to America*, I can remember thinking to myself... We were left feeling somewhat apprehensive about the whole track competitions after that.

Sat in the start house moments before the start of the 2002 road world championships time trial in Germany.

So race day came and first up was the kilometre TT, again like from a few years back the calculations of laps would differ based on the 400-metre track so two and a half laps it was to be. Just a really strange feeling over such a short distance because it alters your ride totally with there not being as many corners and bankings to use for acceleration, but it's the same for everyone so you just have to get on with things. I picked up a silver medal that day just behind my teammate Darren. The next event was to be the team sprint, at just 750 metres for this event it was only actually one lap and 350 metres extra and because the distance is shared equally between the three riders in the team we had to change in one of the bankings which was quite tricky, just a really odd pattern for the event. Nevertheless, we came away with the gold medal which was something that I hadn't achieved in a couple of years at international level.

This for me was a turning point, something that I had been looking for since becoming a full-time athlete. My pro career had started with three gold medals at European level but I had hit a drought ever since and I couldn't understand why until now. I was obviously going through a development phase where in some cases you have to go through a period of time to allow your body to adapt to the different techniques of training that I was doing but didn't in fact realise the knock-on effect that it would have.

After the track events were over, we had two days before we travelled up to new London Connecticut for the road events, we dropped into Manhattan to do a bit of sightseeing before the long journey north. We would be staying on a college campus for the remainder of the trip which was very basic. I can't describe how shit the accommodation was. To give you a small flavour, the room

I was staying in just had a bed in it and we had access to a shared bathroom area with all the other competitors which was like stepping into a mosquito infested cavern! It really was that bad I tell you, no lie! Whilst we were on our gap days it came on the news about the terrorist attack in London on the underground, I can remember being sat in the food area of the campus when I heard this and thinking that this is almost a déjà vu moment with what had happened the last time I was at a European championships. It freaked me a little because again all the talk was about that and it rekindled memories of that day in 2001. Obviously, this went on for a few days and then you realise that you have to get your head back into the game.

So the road events came and went with no real success for myself as I punctuated in the road race and spent 40 minutes pulling my ring out in the pissing rain trying to get back on to the bunch that were traveling at such a high pace that even when I was using the team car to sit behind to try and get some assistance, it still wasn't going to make up that gap that I had lost.

Straight after the race we had the mammoth task of packing everything and driving back south to JFK and the flight home, I can clearly remember falling asleep as soon as I got seated on the plane. Out like a light I went, I can recall feeling all cosy and warm, drifting with the sound of the engines and movement of the plane, so nice it was, hours just in a deep sleep to then wake up and realise that we were still on the ground and still taxiing out to the runway. How was this possible I can remember thinking, surely I had been asleep for hours and we were almost home, but no, we were still on the runway in a queue waiting, so I went from the joy and comfort of a deep sleep to now realising that I was still seven hours from home and even worse becoming wide awake and in a mood because we had only travelled less than a mile from the terminal when I thought I had been asleep for hours. Shit happens, needless to say that the rest of the flight was shit.

On my return I think I took a week off of training and then we had around six weeks until the European track championships over in Alkmaar, Holland. We travelled on the boat to Holland which I tell you is the shittiest way to travel anywhere; cramped and very tiring, oh and to be woken up en masse by an announcement on the ship's public address system has to be the worst thing ever.

The main reason for me being at this event was that we were targeting the team sprint, after the Athens Paralympic Games it was identified that I should have actually been selected as it would have enabled the team to be represented in this event at the games and possibly coming out of it with a medal, but it was something that had been overlooked at the time of selection but was brought to light in recent months. So now the focus had switched to this event and working towards winning it at every available competition.

With this in mind and having won a few months back at the CP world championships we wanted a clean sweep, race day came and we had a great run in qualifying. The event was run as an open European championship, that also mention that other nations from around the globe could enter, so like non-European. In the final we were up against the USA, we won the event but were later relegated to 2nd place due to an infringement of the rules based on where a rider could move and change for the following rider to come through. At first, we were a bit pissed to say the least, but then because it was the USA that were gifted the win. We did in fact still win the European title so it was a little bit silly on the event organisers' part because this was in a European championship, a bit of a loophole in the rules at the time. So that was it for me, I was straight on to a plane and home, no boat this time, don't think I could have stuck it to be honest, may have thrown myself overboard...

2006 was another shit year, bad luck all round, at the start of the year I suffered with a bad spell of saddle sores that would not clear up and really hampered my riding, then I was knocked from my bike by three youths just stepping out into the road in Manchester which resulted in me suffering concussion after hitting the road pretty hard, destroying my helmet and leaving me pretty shook up and off the bike for almost two weeks, then a few months later I suffered from tachycardia whilst out riding. It was the scariest thing I have suffered health related. I was nearing the end of a four-hour training session on the road when I was stopped at a set of traffic lights. I noticed I was becoming slightly short of breath. I looked down at my heart rate monitor and it was reading 189. As I raised my head my visions suddenly went like a tunnel effect with things starting to go very dark, of course I shit myself, not literally but in the space of two or three seconds I thought of everything that I had ever done and also thought is this it, is this where it happens, suddenly I was gasping for air watching my heart rate all the time, 190, 196, 201. I was stood still yet felt like I was at the end of a race. The last figure I noticed was 206 before I went down on the curb side. I came too and quickly looked again, it was dropping, 160, 136 and then a massive drop to 94 in the space of a second which I felt in the most weirdest of ways. I sat there for a few minutes wondering what had happened, then I stood up and climbed on the bike, it was three or four kilometres to get home and mostly downhill so I slowly carried on home. As soon as I got in I phoned the team doctor and explained to him to which he replied that it sounds like a tachycardia, he said in his doctors laid backed manner that to take it easy over the next few days as it can be pretty common in adults. Of course, why didn't I think of that whilst seeing my heart rate reading 206 whilst stood still. Silly me! In the following weeks it would keep happening until I was hospitalised after just sitting in the chair watching countdown one afternoon when it happened and carried on for about 40 minutes completely tiring me out. After the visit to hospital we identified that there were certain things within my diet that may be contributing to it so we started to analyse what it could be. For months it kept happening which took my eye off everything and just freaked me out to the point that I started to not want to go out of the house, not want to ride my bike, every time I would feel a skip in my heart rhythm or a shortness of breath I would panic, even though it had been explained to me in great depth I was still worried and affected by this.

Often training alone, it's the way I prefer as it allows me to get into my own thoughts and concentrate on the job in hand. Majorca is the preferred base for early season training camps that I've used for most of my career.

The time came for me to get on the plane to fly to Switzerland for the world championships, I was not in the right frame of mind at all. My thoughts were elsewhere, I had a devastating time out in Switzerland, my racing was not what it should have been and I had failed to produce any medals. I only had myself to blame for letting my thoughts run away with me, but it was one of those things that just seem to get a grip and didn't want to let go. On my return I was in a pretty dark place of not knowing what was going to happen regarding my future career nor my health in general. At the end of that year somehow, I was given a chance with my contract to roll into 2007 and focus yet again at meeting the selection for the world championships that were to take place in Bordeaux, France. This was possibly to be my last lifeline before the Paralympic Games to take place in 2008. Still I was having these tachycardia events, albeit they were becoming less and less but it was more the mental side of things that I was struggling with; the uncertainty of when they would happen, was this something that I was going to have to live with for the rest of my life, could I actually live with it and deal with the mental side. I couldn't see any light at the end, I was just going to have to deal with it somehow – easier said than done. We were still looking at things in my diet and we narrowed it down to caffeine or some sort of stimulant that I may be ingesting without even being aware, then we found the one possible thing that it could be: (taurine) an amino sulfonic acid, found in a lot of energy drinks of today that is often combined with caffeine to improve mental performance and mixed with augers and other ingredients that is mixed in a wide range of these drinks which can increase heart rate, elevate blood pressure and cause anxiety plus other long-term symptoms. I looked again at what I had used to consume and at what things I may still be adding to my diet. Sure, enough I pinpointed what it may be and stopped consuming straight away. It took a few weeks but eventually the tachycardia stopped, but mentally I was left with the panic attacks that developed off the back of this happening. They were hard to deal with, even though I now know what caused the initial problem I was now left with another. Mental health is a huge thing to try to deal with and you need to seek help as soon as you can because to try to deal with things on your own is not the correct way, at the time the GB team were starting to invest in sports psychology and the mental approach for athletes at events such as the Olympics. This really helps as I had someone, I could go to chat about these issues that I was having based around panic attacks, we soon got to work but again it was all down to me.

Quite often we go to people, but they can't wave a magic wand, they give you the tools and advise and then it's up to you to put it to action. That's the hard part, putting into action, it means actually doing something that quite often you don't want to. I was now in this very situation, I remember sat in the middle of the Manchester velodrome thinking if I don't do this then I might as well pick my bag up and leave because I isn't going to make the games next year unless I get over this. And with that I started to work hard, I still kept getting the panic attacks, even when I got on the plane to Bordeaux I had one but I wasn't going to let it ruin my chances.

The team sprint day came and I was fully in control, I had done every bit of training I could have, I had worked on my mental approach and dealing with all the issues of the past 12 months or so. I was ready. In the qualifying we were the fastest team and set ourselves up for the final. I rode back to the hotel for a chill, jumped into a cold bath for 20 minutes and then into my compression wear and then into bed for two hours sleep. I then had a small bit to eat and rode back to the velodrome. My dad had travelled up from Spain to watch the racing so he was sat in the stands, we did the routine warm up and the scene was set. I was running man one, my bike was loaded into the gate, but as I climbed on to the bike I realised that the mechanism that should hold the bike firmly in place had not been closed properly, the mechanic, Spike, came over to me and whispered in my ear that to keep still as they had forgotten to tighten the start gate, this meant that I was free to roll at any time, the bike was just being held up by an open seat post clamp. I remember thinking back to a documentary I watched as a 14-year-old where Linford Christie said you should always go on the B of the bang, so here I was, unsecured and could launch away when I chose to, the countdown started and I literally went out of the gate on the last beep!

The rest is history, we won the event, world champions, and if you watch the clip on YouTube you will see the bike move in the gate beforehand and the freedom that I had when the last beep started, you can also witness the mechanic give me the heads up on proceedings.

Just a beautiful ending to what had been a very testing 12–15 months but thanks to everyone that had helped me that year.

So 2008 had appeared and it was all about the games, selection was very hard, the team had only a limited amount of spaces so competition was tight and very stressful but I was selected. I was lying on my bed at home when I got the phone call from Chris Furber, the head coach at the time. I was extremely made up, having not made the games four years earlier, this meant a lot! I flew out to Beijing on my own a few days before the rest of the team as I knew I would suffer with the jet lag and I didn't want it to drag on in to the start of the games. On arrival I was greeted by a guide that put me in a taxi and we proceeded to downtown Beijing and to a hotel where I met up with our team manager. She asked me if I was hungry to which I replied, "Starving." I'd just stepped off of a nine-hour flight so I could eat anything at that point, we ended up in some noodle bar which I must say was just a delight; the food was out of this world. I found that I couldn't stop eating it. What was more noticeable was the way that the Chinese people would sit and consume their food, just fascinating, you need to see it to believe it; very uncouth, but that's culture for you.

So my first games, it was massive, huge! It was quite hard to deal with all the athletes from all the sports from all over the world in one place. Busy would be an understatement. It would eventually crack me up, but first the racing. I was here just for the one event, the kilometre TT, the team sprint that I was part of 12 months earlier I had not met the selection times for so I was just entered for this one event. The velodrome was amazing, the design and everything about it was breath-taking. Speaking of breath-taking my panic attacks were no more now, having worked really hard on my mental approach since 2007 up to now. With race days just around the corner my family had arrived in town and I met up with them in some random street by complete accident whilst out riding. It was great to see them and we had a little chat and stuff but obviously I needed to be back in the confines of the Olympic village before dark.

So race day, I just ran through the normalities of the warmup and then just a case of putting the race suit on and getting set. Unfortunately when we came to find my race suit, because they were all packed and kept together secretly it turned out that my two made to measure suits had in fact been left in Manchester, so there I was, all warmed up ready to go, had prepared myself both physically and mentally over the past 12 months let's say for the biggest sporting event of my life to find that my top secretly developed race suits were 8100km away, *terrific!* With no time to question why or who had ballsed up, the staff rallied around and located a suit that I could get into. I don't know to this day whose it was but the arse end was a bit baggy in it. Nevertheless it helped me to my first Paralympic Games medal which was a huge achievement when I look back over the previous couple of years that I may not have even been here due to my results being up and down at times.

That's it, I was actually able to call myself a Paralympian, and with all that came the engagements with the queen and prime mister etc., things that as a kid you would never had thought that you would do or be part of. I mean I recall dancing with Tony Blair's wife at some function in Manchester. But hay ho! That's life!

The next Olympic cycle I was taking a different approach, I was going to ride on the road for a few sessions, something different and a bit more endurance conditioning work. 2009 was ill of travelling, I mean a horrendous amount, with training camps and racing I calculated it to be around almost five months away from home spread out over the race season, it was again to be a building year, going from track sprint to road endurance required a lot of adjustment both in training and diet. As a track sprinter I was weighing in at 72–74 kilos as race weight whereas at my best road season I was at 58 kilos race weight so it was a big shift to start but gained some great results. In 2009 I had pushed myself up to finishing in the top five at world championships road time trials and road race. 2010 was for me to be nothing less than podium finishes. In April 2010 whilst out in northern Spain at a stage race, I was involved in a crash where half the bunch came down in some pretty tough weather conditions. I ended up on the other side of a road barrier. I was able to get back on but struggled for the rest of the race. A few days later we arrived in the south of France for another stage race where I was feeling sick and couldn't get things together, I completed the event but with no spectacular result. Two weeks after arriving home I found out that I did in fact brake my wrist in that accident almost a month ago, the hospital put me in a cast and sent me on my way for six weeks they said. I was mortified because I knew that in just two weeks' time it was to be the first World Cup event in Segovia, Spain. This was a race that I had targeted for the start of the year but with me having broken the wrist and in a cast, it seemed like it wouldn't happen.

Beijing 2008 Paralympic Games podium. Silver in the 1km TT.

After a lengthy phone call from the hospital car park to my coach Chris Furber and begging him to put me on that plane in two weeks' time even with a cast on my arm, I managed to convince him to do so. On arrival at the event and once settled into the hotel, I got to work on the road time trial course. It wasn't the most comfortable thing to do but my head was well in the game and had been for months for this event. I rode over the course hour after hour working out every bump, every stone and the fastest lines to take whilst trying to support my left arm, which is my best arm, in the cast. The evening before the race I went to see the mechanic to see if he could alter my plaster in any way, it was up to my elbow so my movement was limited. We came to the idea that we could cut a bit off and then gaffer tape parts of it to cut down on the aero drag in theory. It sounded great and we had this awesome picture in our minds. To this day I don't know if his picture was the same as mine but it worked. I produced my best performance ever, even to today's standards I don't think I have performed as well as I did on that day to take the win by some margin. I remember the last three kilometres heading into the small village where the finish was, it was so fast yet I was thinking in slow motion as if I was just hitching a ride and watching everything pass by. What a day, the day I turned over the late great Javier Otxoa, the ex-Tour de France rider that I learnt so much from in my time racing against him. RIP my friend!

At the world championships later that year in Canada I was placed 4th in the road time trial and I think the same in the road race but I'm unsure to be totally honest.

Team sprint final at the 2005 Paralympic world cup in Manchester, I was always the gate man up until the 2012 Paralympic games where I rode 2nd man.

Top spot on the podium after a Stella ride with team mates Mark and Darren.

With the shift in discipline over the past few years 2011 was the year to start focusing on what I was going to be targeting for the 2012 games. I wanted to target the endurance events as that is what I had been doing now and building towards but again 2011 was a shit year. I collected two medals at the track world championships in Italy in the March but come the road world championships in the September out in Denmark I wasn't selected for the road time trial but just for the road race which was a really tough ask with the pedigree of riders in the mix and I hadn't really focused my training on the road race.

So at the end of 2011, I was dropped from the Great Britain team, my contract would be honoured until the March of 2012 and that was it. I was in yet a really dark place, my dream of competing in front of a home crowd at the Paralympic Games had taken a massive blow, I didn't know where to turn. Was that it, was it all over? I'd hit a depression, I eventually got myself hooked on prescription painkillers and was slowly going downhill. Christmas had come and gone and something made me get back on the bike. I was still contracted until March so I put a training programme together and got myself fit again. At the end of February, I received a phone call from the GB team manager asking me in for a meeting. Initially I thought it was just like a close of contract type of thing, but no, they were asking me back, they had hit a stumbling block with the team sprint and needed a man, one to possibly ride the team in the London games. *Shit*, I thought as I was sat there. I was struggling to take this in. I told them that in two days' time I would be getting on a plane for a pre-planned three-week training camp that I was going on, they pretty much said that they needed me. I'm a massive team player and to be asked something of this importance who's going to say no, I took the offer and that was that, I spent the next three weeks in Spain training behind a motor scooter for three to four hours a day. Once I arrived back in the UK, the GB team ran some tests on my fitness and all different types of monitoring to find that I was in the shape of my life. We then ran the pre-games training camp and went into the qualification period. Right at this point my dad had caught a virus and was quickly rushed to hospital where he was placed in an induced coma, this was pretty bad. I remember receiving the call at 10 o'clock in the evening and then driving the 60 miles to the hospital he was at, With the other medical conditions that my dad had, the doctors were preparing us for the worst. Literally the next few hours could change everything. Suddenly we were all thrown into the disarray, no one knew what to think or say; time would only tell the outcome.

After I few days at the hospital I returned to training in Manchester. it wasn't easy but I had to stay focused. As time went by there was no sign of the hospital bringing him out of the coma. We had camp coming up that was in London that the selection process would be taken from so we would need to set sometimes that would be looked at and then selection would be made from that outcome. It was a difficult time as I was on the phone most days worrying but I had to concentrate on putting down some good times as well for the selectors.

The days came and went and we returned home having done everything that was required of us, it was just a case of waiting now. During the waiting time my dad was eventually brought out of the induced coma and started the long road to recovery.

It was now June time and I was in my car driving from a school that I had been giving a talk to when I received a call. It was from my team manager at the time, he was calling to say that I had been selected for the games in London. There was not a lot I could do sat behind the wheel at 95 kilometres per hour, except grip the wheel even tighter in excitement. I can't tell you how much that one phone call meant to me, everything that I and the family had gone through in the past few months and even back as far as 2011 – it was just amazing news.

In the weeks that followed it was all about preparing ourselves and putting the finishing touches to the team sprint. My dad was making progress in his recovery so everything was moving in the right direction. Life has this tendency to just throw up things when you least expect it, quite often presenting you with the most testing times. Now we can either lay down and let it beat us or we can stay standing and deal with it. We may not like what we are faced with and it may bring more shit as we stand there but eventually, we will succeed. We just have to persevere with it because that's what will make us stronger!

So the games came, and what a game it was, words can't describe it. My dad was well enough to attend and see our race, the weather was the best the country had seen, the crowds were amazing and the organisation was second to none. My only gripe is I came away with a silver medal and not the gold that we had set out to achieve, but I suppose that's elite sport these days. The margins are so close 0.65, I think it was between gold and silver that day. Oh, well, we live and learn. So what's next, who knows, I like to have a go again and possibly go the one better so I'll keep this space open just in case. No regrets hey!

A crisp spring day in 2019 as I begin my 2020 Paralympic Games comeback campaign after a somewhat difficult period of my life with mental health issues.

My last major win in 2017 before taking a break from the sport, a twelfth
national championships jersey of my career.

London 2012 Paralympic Games team sprint, I'm sandwiched between my
team mates as a ran second man.

A very disappointing second place by less than a second that was clearly
visible as I held back the emotion and frustration of missing out on Gold on home soil.

Chapter 8
Peddling Politics

Like everything in life, even just pushing the peddles on a bike has politics from the clothing you wear, to Olympic selection, with both carrying the same level of importance. You're probably wondering to yourself how can politics on clothing come anywhere near politics at Olympic selection? That will be the 'marginal gains' that have been banded around for many years now. It's the small cogs that drive the bigger gears that can ultimately win you the biggest prize of them all.

My first encounter with any sort of politics in bike racing was back in the very early days of 2003. Paracycling was such a small movement that you could have wrote the rules on a postage stamp, the GB programme didn't even have a manager for a good proportion of that season after the previous candidate was relieved from the posting at the end of 2002 due to 'having it away' with a female rider apparently. We were just sort of left to our own devices as to what we were actually meant to be doing until around the June time when it was announced that we would being going to a European championships at the end of August in the Czech Republic. We were obviously expected to deliver a sack full of medals. Needless to say that with around six weeks' notice my form was a little shabby of where it should have been heading towards a championship, and of course, I was held responsible for not being in top shape. I remember sending a strongly worded email to Sir Dave Brailsford in the early part of 2003, pointing out that the para programme riders had just been cast to one side and forgotten about for months. I was at this point fairly new to the emailing world and didn't think twice before sending the unedited 'say it from the heart' version. In fact, it was such a rough copy that it basically slagged off the entire set up of the world class performance programme at the time, that was still pretty much in its infancy. I was lucky that Dave is quite an understanding guy and was able to see through my lack of education.

In the following season was of course Paralympic year, we had a guy that was, shall we say, 'babysitting the team', and I say that very loosely. I wouldn't say that he carried many skills as a manager, but such a nice person that you would struggle to even think about losing your temper with him in your moments of frustration, the sort of guy that would help anyone at a jumble sale, but I suppose for the four or five riders that were part of the paracycling programme back then, it didn't really require someone with a huge skill set. Just someone to dish out the sweets as we crossed the finish line really.

I remember thinking at the time that my days as a club rider were of a better standard, asking for a new inner tube one day was commented back by 'haven't you a puncture repair kit', seriously! I had visions of us riding the Paralympic road race with panniers and mudguards.

In the selection process for the 2004 Paralympics he unfortunately overlooked the team sprint event, which left the GB team missing out on a gold medal opportunity, which was only brought to management's attention just a few days before the actual event when an interim manager was flown out to Greece following the melt down that this other guy was having. They had of course not selected me for the Paralympics, so didn't have a team formation to put together anyway. The international paracycling stage as a whole was a lacklustre movement in them days, most of the events you could have actually rode in trainers whilst waving a flag around, 'that's how bad it was'. Fortunately, things have picked up slightly, they use a stopwatch now as opposed to an egg timer, though some events can give you the feeling that a calendar is needed if I'm totally honest.

The world championships in 2006, that's when my anxieties started to really surface. For almost 12 years they had lay dormant, untroubled with stresses and pressure until now. I would always be a little pissed off with situation sometimes not going right in training or at races, but these championships got the better of me. They would provide a grow bag environment, a greenhouse that the future of my international cycling career would live in, feeding off a genetically modified fertiliser spread around by a broken watering can.

For twelve months prior to the worlds, my training programme had been geared towards the team sprint and the one-kilometre TT, where it had been identified that my strengths were at. The outcome of the team sprint at that particular event in agile Switzerland was that the team sprint was disqualified for breaking the rules during the race by moving offline before the change box. This was such a stupid error by the team selectors to not have selected me. I had ran all the formation sessions, taken part in all of the drills that we had done in the lead up to flying out, and then for them to select somebody that resided overseas for the majority of the season, it just didn't make sense. Up until that point the team had been undefeated in all the previous events. I was approached in the minutes following that disqualification on race day by a senior member of staff that said, "If you had been in that team set up then we would have won." Not the sort of thing that you need rubbing in your face, and rather late when they didn't select me at the trial which took place two days earlier. It was ringing bells that I had heard before after the Athens games buffoonery, my anxieties crept in, slowly sending me thoughts of the hours of training, the formation runs that we had done in the previous months in the run up to the event. To witness that mess up didn't make sense. Team GB had invested heavily in myself with the type of training and everything else that went with it yet left me out when it mattered. Of course I was to blame for not making the selection but had their selection process also been a catalyst for losing out.

On my return home from that event I started to struggle with things. Like everyone else I was just trying to get on in life, but life gets tough sometimes, I just kept thinking about the time that I had put into the relentless training which the coaches and other staff had constructed, as well as witnessed the time and commitment that had been placed on this one discipline by myself. I say all this, and it is in no way a bad reflection on the guy that rode instead of myself. The selectors just had their heads up their arse and didn't see the bigger picture, it just mystified me for some time after.

All this was running wild in my head. I relied heavily on funding to do what I did, half of the things you go through as an athlete you never really tell people. You know I had all sorts of problems over the years from eating disorders to substance use that were all brought about by the pressures of trying to do the right thing. It's not something that I am proud of but the pressures that you were put under were ridiculous, but I was in such a state, I was blaming myself for other people's decisions, asking myself the questions that I couldn't answer, I have a passion for my sport that no one was going to come between. I would look in the mirror and hate what looked back at me, all I would see was a damaged body from my childhood accident that wasn't giving me what I needed to produce in training or racing. I started to self-harm, it would just start by scratching myself with sharp objects, then as time went on, I was trying different things. I was living with Natalie, my wife at the time. She would go away a lot with British swimming so it was fairly easy to conceal any wounds from her that I was inflicting on my body. The whole pressure coming out of the GB Squad at the time was like you could not afford to be weak, it was all about positive attitudes, staying focused and not affecting others around you. If it was seen that your attitude was not that of their thinking then you could very easily find yourself on the outside of the circle. Even when they started working with sports psychologists you still felt that you were unable to divulge your true feelings for fear of it being mentioned in debrief meeting between senior staff and leadership teams, you felt that you were being scrutinised on every single aspect. It was obvious that the GB Team were trying to build a medal factory. You would hear it all of the time. Slowly it started to fester, it was no longer a podium programme, gold is all that they wanted with no consideration for people's mental health and wellbeing.

Somehow I was able to hide what I was doing, each day after I had harmed I would fear other riders catching sight of the marks, but if I'm totally honest, I think a lot of them had reached the point in their own minds as of the pressures they were feeling that they didn't care about anyone else but themselves. The idiotic ways in which the senior staff would place unnecessary pressure on riders was that of delusion, they would try to portray this massive feeling of a team spirit, when really it was far from that. I recall one world championships where we were treated like robots as soon as we arrived, being told that we needed to boss the track in our scheduled training sessions to scare the other nations. Just pathetic! The racing showed that just how good a nation we were, we didn't need to show off in training for the sake of some coach's ego. No one would ever speak out about such things for fear, you just felt you needed to shut up and put up. If you had a bad race and didn't come away with the gold medal it was like it was the end of the world, you would be blanked even if you had walked away with say a silver or a bronze, of course everyone wants to win, it's only natural that you're going to be disappointed, but you were scarcely noticed should you not have reached the top spot. You would feel the tension as you sat in your chair trying to console yourself amidst the organised chaos that surrounded the pits of the velodrome, the shiftiness and avoidance of eye contact of staff passing you as they came in and out of the pits making you feel ever so more uncomfortable was an unbearable thought that you knew would be part of the routine for anyone not hitting the top peg. The enjoyment of racing a bike was lost, the enthusiasm drained from you by attitudes that had been programmed to accept only one outcome. I was racing at a level that many dream of, but only the few have the ability to be part of, but was I now part of a seemingly X factor type reality show that was taking a hold on the sporting world.

In the year prior to the Beijing games we flew to Australia for a training camp, the Australian national track championship, followed by a stopover in Beijing on our return for some testing. The big topic of conversation amongst athletes across all sports was the so-called air pollution that was being made into a huge issue in the media. The talk was that everyone was going to need an inhaler for the duration of the Olympic and Paralympic Games. Where the idea of using an inhaler came from, I will never know, but this was to be the subject in the lead up to the games. I didn't see the point to be honest, I had never suffered from asthma whatsoever throughout my life, so where were the gains to be made here. Was this for real, or was there something else in this idea? It got to the stage where it was all that athletes were talking about, we went through lung function testing while in Beijing on our stop over to measure any effects of the air quality, and who would possibly benefit from having an inhaler. I could see myself that this all seemed a bit sketchy, or rather a loophole that somebody had seen as maybe an advantage somewhere along the line. The inhaler is governed by the TUE system which allows athletes with certain conditions that require medication to be able to administer the drug/drugs under a controlled banner, but why were athletes that had never suffered from effects of asthma now being targeted, or rather offered the use of the inhaler. I certainly didn't think the environmental air quality warranted such an extreme level to go to. I queried it at the time, the only answer that I was given was that it may or may not assist your breathing.

The term (exercise-induced asthma) was used, though from my understanding of tests that have been carried out in previous years the result from cyclists that have shown signs of 'exercise-induced asthma' comes from when a cyclist is breathing cold air when a contraction of the airways brings a feeling of a tight chest, but instead it is caused by rapid and heavy breathing during exertion, plus atmospheric factors can exacerbate this which show similar symptoms to that of classic asthma, but this then begged the question that the atmospheric conditions were far from cold during the Beijing games so what would be the point. It was never really elaborated on more than that. I made the decision not to have one purely based on the fact that I had never had asthma. Whether other athletes at the time took up the idea I don't know, I can only speak for myself. Later on I found out that during the Beijing games roughly 17% of cyclists and around 19% of swimmers were diagnosed with 'asthma', the asthmatic athletes went on to win around 29% of the 33% of medals in those sports, respectively, at the 2012 games in London, out of 10000 competing athletes approximately 700 were confirmed asthma diagnoses and surprisingly, they were almost twice as likely to win a medal as their non-asthmatic peers. Was I right to not use an inhaler, or should I have rolled with the trend, it may have been the difference, but I suppose I will never know.

Obviously in 2007, I was part of the team sprint that went on to win the world championships in emphatic style producing a world record on the way to really seal it, but in 2008 and with it being games year, things seem to go a little crazy. The coaches at the time had me working a lot in the gym. Not only had my workload doubled to that of 2007, but my body weight skyrocketed, adding 13 kilos to my mass. I knew this wasn't a good thing, but I felt the pressure that I had to do what they said or I would be outed and I didn't want to place myself in a situation where I was not selected because of my attitude. I lost my reaction speed from the start gate as I had more weight to shift. In my case with my neurological disability to factor in I was unable to fire up that extra muscle mass so it was counterproductive. So frustrating because I had spent a lot of time in the gym through a huge part of 2008 and in the run up to the games. To not benefit from it was hard to deal with, in 2007 at the world championships I was 59 kilos total body mass. A year later rolling into team sprint trials for the Beijing Paralympic Games I was weighting in at 72 kilos, but could not equate that to a faster time from the start gate, all those hours in the gym just wasted, I felt the energy just drain from me. 13 extra kilos to try to get off the line; in theory it should have produced something. Yeah, my legs looked bigger, other riders were commenting how good I looked, strong and stuff, but that was as far as it went, I look back at that a lot, it amazes me just how the coaches got it so wrong, if in 2007 I produced a world record with the body comp that I had, then why mess with it to the tune of 13 extra kilos. Perhaps I was naive, maybe I should have made more of a conscious effort to have input, but again you were in this mentality that you felt that you couldn't really question anything. I suppose I was leaving it in the hands of the experts, this obviously isn't in any way aimed at any particular coach, looking at things they were young, trying to climb the ladder. I think now maybe that they were seeing what the Olympic guys were doing in their training and preparation, then trying to apply it to the Paralympic riders.

Depending on the disability of the athlete would depend on how it would affect their physiology make up, and whether training technics should have been more tailored to the individual. I just feel it was standard stuff, and whilst for the majority it was working, for me it was plunging me into a world of questions about myself which led me to depressive state of fear which turned into my eating disorder.

The following year I decided to coach myself, I felt that it was the only way that I was going to be able to find myself, and relight my passion, belief and try to rekindle some self-esteem.

At the Beijing games in the days that followed my kilo event I self-harmed due to the politics that where going on at the time that surrounded the team sprint selection and just the track side of racing in general. It was embarrassing from a point of view of the staff, but I ended up taking it out on myself, it was half the reason why I ended up leaving the games early for fear that I may have hurt someone.

I felt relief from the misery of the pressure once I had cut myself, but that would only last until the next moment of turmoil and having that association with the track I needed to move away from it for the time being.

2009 was a learning curve, I took a few spills on the road, early season in late February, we went over to France where we raced a short four-day stage race where I finished third on the first stage, but then crashed in the wet on the second day. A few days later we drove into northern Spain where my role was a domestic, working for my then teammate Darren Kenny, that again was just really learning the ropes. We started to build a good relationship on the road, we had a big year of travelling from race to race around Europe, quite a few training camps and things were gelling well. The road world championships were in Italy in the September which I was really looking forward to. My form was the best it had ever been. I finished 4th in the road time trial, my best international road result to date, all the top five riders were within minutes of each other. The road race a few days later was to be a day where I had to stick to the plan of the domestic, even though I had the form to win the race. I had to put my own ambitions on hold, just do my job. It worked perfectly; my teammate nailed the win leaving me to roll in with a 4th place. I felt amazing, and what was really evident was the fact that mentally I'd had a season free of harming myself and any sort of anxieties.

After spending a lot of time in Spain chasing my dad around on a motor scooter for three and four hours a day in the region of Murcia, I began to re-focus, as I was determined to make an impact on the 2010 road season with targeting a few World Cups.

I asked the national Squad for a bit more support with equipment, and just some general backing, Chris Furber was one of the guys that is a great guy to use as a sounding board with a wealth of experience, a little enthusiastic when he first started with our programme, I seem to remember he joined us for the first time during a training camp in Majorca, January 2006, 'all guns blazing in his first speech'. I recall all the riders just looked at each other as if to say, "who did they say this guy was". Funny times, I'm sure he won't blink an eye at me mentioning it…

A fall with half the bunch whilst out at a stage race in Spain wasn't the best start to my campaign which left me with a broken wrist, and with the first World

Cup just weeks away I had to beg Chris Furber to let me be part of the team that would fly to the event. Even though I had a cast on my arm, fortunately he recognised the hard work that I had put in and selected me. I finished a strong 6th in the road race only to go on to win the road time trial a few days later. It was a massive thing for me to achieve, not only had I got the training right, but I had also overcome the demons of previous years that had trampled my self-esteem.

I must admit I was nervous going out there, I put a lot of pressure on myself as I wanted to win that one event so much. I also knew that I was up against things as I had struggled in the run up to get comfortable in my time trial position due to my arm being in a cast.

I took massive confidence from this, but unfortunately the rest of that season went a bit to the wall.

Again other people becoming 'enthusiastic' at the prospect that I could win the worlds to the point that they said it will be good to race an event that they were hosting towards the back end of the season wearing the world champion skin suit. They had already put the medal around my neck, the promises of some lightweight equipment that would be added to my bike didn't materialise. It was a bitter blow, but what happened next was a bit more of an insult.

The talent identification programme that had been developed in order to fast track athletes had taken on a handful of riders that had funds pumped into them in order to progress forward to the 2012 games in London, obviously this was a massive deal for UK sport which the national Squad needed to show that the programme worked. After my World Cup win in 2010 and the time between the world championships later that year the team shifted their focus on to another rider that was on this talent programme. The support towards myself became less to what had been prior to my World Cup win, this was noticeable. As we approached the world championships I felt no confidence whatsoever, Thinking back now they had put the world championship gold medal around my neck after the World Cup win and decided to put their focus into the talent programme riders as they needed to show some sort of progression for the last few years of government and public funding stream. I remember sitting in the start house as the clock in front of me ticked down for my start not feeling it at all. 'What gear was I even in,' I asked myself. I looked down and I was in the small chainring, not my usual self. Everybody knows that for a time trial you start in the outer ring unless it's a hill climb, my punchiness and aggressive starting position just wasn't there, mentally I was beat, I finished 4th, just 10 seconds away from the podium – pissed off was an understatement. I returned to the UK feeling robbed, I questioned myself thinking it was all my doing, when really the staff that were around me at the time had just lost their focus thinking that it was a done deal after the world cup win.

This feeling would in fact eat away at me for the next twelve months. I struggled to recovery feeling that I had been somehow pushed out for some reason. In 2011, things just became a series of going through the motions. I had returned to the track as we were in the process of chasing points for places at the London games so the team needed as many riders as possible, the track worlds were out in Italy in the march, I just rode around with no intent, somehow coming away with two medals from the pursuit and kilo, certain staff members had just lost interest which was obvious as soon as we stepped off the plane. The GB team just wanted to show that funding from their talent programme wasn't being wasted to which there was so much more enthuses placed on that programme than the world class riders themselves. I remember totally losing it during my bronze medal ride for the pursuit when I chopped the front wheel as I caught my opponent and exchange some toilet talk as he pushed me wide when I went around him. I was so angry that day that I just rode straight into the pits, packed my bag and went back to the hotel. I was ignored for pretty much the rest of the trip, I felt in such a dark and lonely place that I can remember insulting people, ranting on Twitter and just being totally out of character, acting without taking responsibility. Had I really been driven to these depths of sheer carelessness, but yeah, I just didn't care. I was asked to be the backup rider for the team sprint which I reluctantly took part in. Deep down I'm a team player, but that day I wanted to tell them where to go. Even that event was a farce in its selection, they knowingly ran a team formation that was not even going to be possible for the following year at the Paralympic Games, as the points system was to change for the riders that you were going to be allowed to ride. So them running the setup that they had made no sense at all. They had adopted the saying "life's not fair", it was used so many times that I think they had all received a laminated version that they carried around in their wallets as a reminder of the culture that they were now part of. Each time you would see the sports psychologist that's all they would say after each session, you never really got the answer or direction that you were looking for. It was an almost CBA culture with no one wanting responsibility for anything.

August of that year brought the tipping point; after winning the national time trial championships I went and spent three weeks in Spain training behind a scooter in temperatures between 35 and 45 degrees in order to elevate my fitness before flying to Denmark for the road world championships. I was feeling in the best shape ever, having put the disappointment of the last 12 months behind me yet again I was dealt a blow a few days before the worlds time trial, they decided that I wasn't to ride the time trial. I couldn't believe that they had left it right up until we were actually out at the event, I had put so much into training, I was on blistering form for this one event to then be overlooked yet again. This just completely finished me, they tried to say that they were focusing me for the road race, but with no actual results in any road races over that season, how they showed evidence of that to selectors I don't know, especially with all my best results coming from just time trials, it didn't make sense apart from one theory, that being that they wanted their talent programme rider to look better by not having me ride. There were two slots for that event, which they filled the other with my good teammate Darren Kenny. The whole thing was corrupt, they knew that Kenny wasn't on his best form and by riding him instead of myself they were sure of protecting their investment, that being the talent programme rider. In the months that followed I was handed a three-month notice of my programme funding coming to an end, and therefore my London 2012 Paralympic dreams being shattered.

It was almost unimaginable; it was as if I had seen it coming for the past 12 to 18 months. I couldn't really see a way back, the controlling dominator of the management structure at the time was a force that you could not win against in any meeting. The fear of opening your mouth against anyone was a complete no no! The GB team had obviously done the math and knew roughly just how many places they would have for male riders to be part of the team to which they obviously decided on a pecking order which had to include a couple of their talent programme riders. After the news that I had been dreading of, my funding ended. I knew that I wasn't going to be able to just walk into another career just like that, in the initial weeks I berated myself. I did a spectacular demolition job of my own beliefs and passion for the sport, I worked extremely hard at hiding my anxieties and frustrations from the whole family. I have never been one to drink or even like it and could not see the point in taking that route, instead I formed a habit for codeine, the quick fix that would see me through my days. I knew that I was doing wrong, but I couldn't see any way through the horrific emotions that I was feeling. The habit lasted for around three months, fighting my way through the days hoping that no one would notice my changed character, I would lie in bed most nights unable to shut my eyes, but in some way that was far better than lying there thinking of the turmoil that I had been dealt in the past months. I found myself at the point where I would be downing the stuff like it was sugar, I knew at some point that I needed to get a grip on myself before somebody found out, that then brought on a whole new dimension of anguish, circle after circle. I was just spinning with nowhere to go. The one love and passion for riding a bike that delivered such a rush when I first started at the age of 14 was now becoming my demise, it was only a matter of time before the self-destruct button would be hit. With my wife being well on track at British swimming to represent at the London games, I had to take a hold of my situation and in the January of 2012 after I worked out that my funding would end on March 31st 2012 I knew I needed to get myself right physically, but most of all mentally.

I buggered off to Spain for three weeks in the January to do a big block of some quality work behind the scooter. The weather was dyer and very unseasonal for the local area with heavy rain, flooding and low temperatures, but I couldn't let it stop play. I couldn't afford to waste any time hanging around, I wanted one last assault at trying to get to the games. The very first session I will never forget, I'm sure I died that day, or the old version of me did... It was 6 degrees; a howling bitter wind blew from the north bringing horizontal rain of which was mostly behind us for the first few hours as I chased my dad who was riding the scooter at a constant 40kmph. After covering close on 80 kilometres in a southerly direction and then over to the west through the twisting mountainous countryside we had reached the town of Cartagena, as we slipped on to the RM-F35, a pan flat road that runs from Cartagena to San Javier for almost 30 kilometres through a farming region, the brutal weather suddenly hit us with its full force, the road surface would disappear beneath the torrent of water that was dropping from the sky mixed with the orange coloured soil that would be streaming from the saturated fields that lined each side of the route. My eyes focused on the exhaust pipe of the scooter as the spray would be hitting it, but then in an instant be evaporated from the heat that the exhaust was giving off. My hands numb and face battered by the conditions I was reduced to tears; emotions were kicking me from all directions. I was losing sight of things, unable to pick out the road below I found myself in a somewhat outer body experience, feeling nothing but sheer anguish. I had lost the back wheel of the scooter and felt orphaned amongst the abandoned fields. All I wanted to do was stop and drop to my knees, but I knew that if did, then that would have been the end. The faint rear light of the scooter had disappeared into the mist leaving me alone. As the bike rolled to a stop, I climbed off, stood feet half submerged in mud and water. My head dropped, tears streamed down my face adding to the misery of the day, what had I become? Why had I turned to substance abuse in the previous months? Why was I now here feeling striped raw taking the hit of the elements? Then I spotted a lone bird hopping around at the side of the road, not knowing where it was going or what it was doing. I realised that I was in the same space of time with thoughts of not knowing, but the bird was just getting on with things, unfazed by the conditions. I gathered myself a little and climbed back on, my dad had stopped further up the road, and once I had re-joined him, I said that I couldn't go on. I was broken, dead, nothing to offer. Shaking as I sipped my drink, I could see that my dad also was suffering even with the weatherproof clothing he was wearing. A van driver stopped and offered me a lift as he could obviously see that things weren't right, but something was telling me that I had to go on. I had put myself in this god-awful situation, not just on the day, but also over the past months with the drug habit, maybe this was the point where I rid it of my system. It's a day that will always stay with me, the day that made my 2012 as I beat myself to death, but also broke free. By the end of the three weeks I had covered just over 2000 kilometres. I was absolutely on my knees when I boarded the plane to return home. The most difficult part was being able to stay on the straight and narrow, I had been off the codeine two weeks pre me boarding the plane to Spain. I knew that the training that I had set myself was enough to keep my mind occupied and fatigued enough to not think of anything else. I had one objective in mind, that was to make the team selection for the games.

During my recovery week after returning it was in fact the UCI para track world championships over in Los Angeles. I watched the live stream at some god unearthly hour of the day to catch the racing, the times that came out of those championships were in the ball park of where I was aiming at for a 3km pursuit trial in Manchester that I had pre-arranged. I then caught the result of the team sprint, the pedigree of the team wasn't there anymore, 'I think they finished 3rd.

Two weeks later I received a call from the manager of the team. It came by total surprise asking me into the velodrome for a chat, I was thinking that maybe it was about preparing for my pursuit time, but in fact it was to ask me something very different. They had found themselves in a pickle over the team sprint, and as a result of the new points system that was now in place they didn't have a competitive team, basically asking me back to ride the team sprint for the games! It was a bit of a shock considering they hadn't been interested in me for that event for a number of years, plus now with the added fact that I wasn't interested in that event brought around new complications. I just really wasn't interested whatsoever, I just wasn't thrilled by this offer at all, it had landed totally out of the blue. Basically they were asking me to put aside my own ambitions of the pursuit and the road time trial to concentrate on just one event which was the total opposite of training to what I had just been doing over the previous months. I couldn't give them an answer there and then, it was a big thing that I had to consider. The dark places that I had been over the past couple of months that nobody knew about that had seen me sink to the lowest depths that anyone can go, and all because of these people that were sat in front of me now with a bag of sweets…! It was quite a moment I can tell you! Then a difficult couple of days followed. I thought of nothing else, it was annoying in some ways because I had wrote this event from my mind, it had pissed me off that much in the past with the politics that surrounded it that I never wanted anything to do with it ever again. Now here I was having to decide what way to go, if I had just turned it down that would have really fucked the team as they wouldn't have had a team for the Paralympic Games, that would also have left me in an undesirable position as my trying to qualify for a position in my own right with the pursuit or the road time trial. If I was to accept the position then that would have meant forfeiting my own personal ambitions, so hard but they knew that they had me. I was of course a big team player and they needed me as equally as I needed them. I had no choice, I had to accept. I didn't set a time for the pursuit at the end of March, but I did fly to Spain for a camp that I had pre-arranged where with my endurance training I mixed in some sprint type efforts to get my foot back in. On my return I was scheduled for some testing in the laboratory at the EIS in Manchester, it was a standard ramp test, v02 max with some added sprint efforts to see where I was at, the sub max test was phenomenal. My scores were through the roof to the point that they stopped the test as the lactate numbers were low and were not shifting even after 40 minutes.

The next stop was the London training camp/selection times process, I obviously had to post a time for the team sprint for the paperwork and the selectors. I had observed the other two riders in the months leading up to this point that were down to post times for the pursuit, I knew that at the particular time I was in much better form than either of them, and once they had set their 3km times I asked the coaches could I get up a post a time just for a laugh, as I knew I could have posted a better time than they had set on that particular afternoon, and quite comfortably as well, as the other two were clearly not on form, but I was told no! Even though the coaches knew I would have gone faster than the other two, but you see, if I had posted a time, then the selectors would have had a holy nightmare as one of the other riders was needed to make up the team sprint, therefore leaving the other rider that was part of the talent identification programme for the last three years on the back foot. The same rider that had taken the pecking order over myself for the last couple of world championships as they needed to show progress, so now here we were in a situation that would have put him out right at the last hurdle. Could you imagine how awkward that would have made the National team look, so to keep the paperwork clean I was the one that had to be held back, the politics were again rearing their ugly head, and all because they cocked it up a few years back by thinking that they were being clever, when really the goons in charge at the time could not see the wood for the trees, it stud out a mile as every other rider could see the mistakes.

I'm sure it would have left them in a complete spin had I been allowed to post a time; their heads were all over the show as it was. You could clearly see that the whole pressure was getting to the staff as well, I'm sure they still would have made the same decision when it came to who they selected, but it would have also brought into question their talent programme and how it had been managed.

After the games in the October of 2012 at the rider review meetings that they hold annually I was once again handed a three-month notice of my funding ended. I had no inclination that this was even on the cards, a couple of weeks previous to the meeting I was sent a questionnaire to fill out and outline my ambitions for the next 12 months, plus my goals for the next Paralympic Games in 2016 out in Rio. I specified that I wanted to pick up with my endurance side of things that I had forgone to help them out before the London training camp where I believe that I was in the best possible form of my life. I believed that I was now in a position physically and mentally to push forward towards a world championship road time trial title and then on to the Rio Paralympic Games where I wanted to finish my career off with the gold medal in the same discipline. The discussions in the meeting went sour from the word go, the manager at the time launched a personal attack at my ambitions and everything that I had wrote down in the questionnaire, even after the testing where I produced off the scale numbers that I punched out in the lab all pointed to a new-found level. He still insisted on attacking me personally by stating that because I didn't want to focus on the team sprint, there was no place on the programme for me. I could tell as I sat there that his whole demeanour was that of a person that was frustrated that I wanted to do something that he didn't believe was possible, so therefore he was venting his anger at me. There were a few other people in on that meeting, coaches and the physiologist, but they just sat there like puppets lined up for the show, failing to offer any back up of the data they had on my file from that year. Previous years' pursuit data was mentioned, but they were dredging the bottom of the filing cabinets by going back two and three years as if to be scatting around for negative data to throw into the party.

The numbers don't lie, that's fact, they knew it. What I had done endurance-wise was unbelievable, those were the exact words that the physiologist said to me and the other coaches in the moments that followed that test back in April of

2012. He also said that he had never seen anything like it before, but then chose to say nothing in that meeting and just sat like a rabbit in the head lights.

My time at Team GB came to an end. It was hard to deal with the rejection, the disregard that they showed to the work ethic that I had put in and the ambitious goals that I had set myself to forward my career to 2016, but there you go. You never really accept it, when somebody is clearly judging you not knowing the true facts or the inwardly battles that you may be having with yourself, you just have to go and prove them wrong.

With support from my domestic team Para-T-Paracycling Team I was able to ride a lot of the UCI road world cups over the following few seasons. It was a difficult time, my team supported me financially and arranged everything, I can't thank them enough for their investment. My progression was showing and in 2014 with the Great Britain set up having undergone a staffing change I was called up to represent the country once again at the Spanish round of the World Cup series where I finished 5th in the TT just 15 seconds from the podium and finishing as best GB riders for my category. This really boosted my confidence, reinstalling my self-esteem, but again it was to no avail come selection time for the road worlds. There was defiantly something not right in all of this, it really brought on the anguish; to pull my bollocks out, make the improvements, be the best GB rider in the class in that season, and to do it independently of the world class programme, my endeavours weren't being recognised. It was a few years later that I discovered from a telephone conversation that a strong case was actually put forward to the sectors to have me at the worlds in 2014 but it was rejected, even after a second attempt. On learning this I realised that a way back into the fold of the GB set up for myself was and probably will never happen now, even after a road World Cup podium medal winning ride just six weeks prior to the Rio Paralympic Games wasn't enough to even receive as much as a well done from anyone.

When I look back now at things, it's said that you shouldn't get tied up in politics, especially as an athlete, but you just can't help it; your passion, it's engrained in you like a stick of rock. As athletes you're all chasing the one thing, the one thing that you found when you started your sports for the very first time. It's not the medal, not the jersey, not the handshakes nor the hugs that come after the success of a win, it is in fact a bit more simpler than that. It's the feeling you get when you know that you have achieved, just that happy feeling that we are all looking for, even at my darkest days I was still searching for that happy feeling, but in my clouded desperation, I sourced it in the wrong places.

Chapter 9
Lost in Space

Relationships, yeah, well, not really my thing. I was too much into my bike racing and training to be bothered, I didn't really have time if I'm honest. I was never in the country long enough to (A) find someone, and (B) put the time in required to find any spark. I was never the marrying type, I always said that I would never get married. I developed some really strong feelings for a girl when I was younger, and when that ended it turned me inside out, shedding tears at a young age over a relationship was not something that happened, but this one girl had stolen my heart. I had just turned 18, her name was Rachael, she lived across the other side of town from me, but I was driving by now, had a car, so I was able to come and go as I pleased now, Rachael was 16 at the time and in her final year at school, she lived with a foster family, and we had met through some friends that we used to hang about with at the time. She was a little taller than me which wasn't my normal MO, but she caught my eye and was always there in the background whenever our small groups would meet up. We swiftly got chatting, and then eventually started seeing each other. I was absolutely besotted with her, we were never really apart from what I can recall, went to a lot of places together, and just got on so well. One evening in the summer of that year whilst on our way back from an outing with two other friends we were involved in a car accident after I misjudged a bend in the road on an unlit stretch of carriageway, we were both OK thankfully, but I never really got over the fact that Rachael or both of us could have died that night. I blamed myself for the accident, which in turn put a strain on the way I thought about things. Things were never the same, Rachael seemed to just take it in her stride, but I let it get to me to the point that the relationship ended. It tore me apart, why was I letting things get to me. I suppose when you care for someone so much like I did then you question why did I not take more care on that bend in the road. As time went by, I lost touch with her and didn't see her again. I suppose since that point I wasn't interested in relationships at all, I had of course that odd girl here and there, but nothing that I would say 'yeah I could spend the rest of my life with you'. So, yeah, that was me, flying solo for years, until I met Natalie, yeah actually met a girl and started dating. Well, 'met' is a bit of a loose term, more introduced by a good friend at the time. My friend was a bit of a swimmer, and after stopping at her house in Manchester a few times she threw Natalie's name at me as a possible date just through chatting as you do, they trained together in the pool at the Manchester aquatics centre, so she suggested that we should all go on a date together.

So yeah the first date rocked, well I was going away to Majorca on a two-week training camp the following morning so if it had gone tits up it was the perfect escape, just so happens it was a flip of the above. Things went well, I had the text messaging off to a fine art, my phone had never been in my hand so much, it probably would have been cheaper to buy shares in O2. I think it was worse for Natalie as she flew to South Africa for three weeks a few days before I returned home so it was almost five weeks I seem to remember before we would see each other again. Now what you have to understand is here's me, never the marrying type, wasn't interested at all, but something had caught me here as I was transformed within the first couple of dates, and I wasn't even trying to fight it. Things took their normal course as they do. A few years later, well three to be precise, we got engaged, and then two years after that we got married, but only for it to last six years pretty much to the day.

It's quite a difficult thing for me to talk about, I have never told anyone the exact reason for the breakup, because quite frankly I was ashamed. All I kept thinking about was what other people might have thought. It's not something that you would wish on anyone, but it happened, and I dealt with it the best way that I knew how without causing embarrassment to myself. So there I was one morning, in the chair catching up on some work emails on the iPad, planning some activities for a school visit that I had organised for the following day. With today's technology everything is synced, so phones and all the apps, within a few moments of being hooked up to the Internet a message pinged up via WhatsApp, it was of course the wife's account. As I sat there when a snippet of this message sprung up I could not believe what I was seeing, my stomach sank with fear, I questioned myself whether I should open the full message, or just ignore what I had just seen. Human instinct prevailing I clicked on the App feeling anxious at what I may find, suddenly it was there before my eyes, hitting me like an unsuspecting car in the middle of the night. My whole world just fell apart within a few seconds of reading the first few lines, to try to comprehend what I was reading. It was like nothing I have ever experienced before; it was brutal. The moment when it dawned on me the exact contents, and the meaning of all the messages, but still I didn't want to believe it, they weren't just messages of a flirty nature, they were messages of intent between two people that were obviously involved to a level that would bring into question my awareness of their situation. I was for a few weeks prior to seeing this content waking in the middle of the night and not sleeping very well just in general, but it was obviously being discussed by my wife and whoever this other guy was as he was questioning her as to whether I suspected, and maybe that is what was keeping me awake at night. As I read through even more of this content, I sensed that this was more than just a casual chat as meetings had been arranged and carried out. Natalie was at work that morning as I sat there in tears thinking the worst possible things, remarkably my mind was trying to convince my conscious being to forget what I had seen, and not to act hastily, but I found myself in somewhat of an uncertain space, confused, upset and the feeling of betrayal setting in. Where do I turn, do I confront her when she returns home, or do I ignore it and forget what

I had seen hoping that it will go away. Eventually I picked up the phone and called my father-in-law. I was shaking, my fine motor skills are not the greatest at the best of times, but by now they were uncontrollable. Even with the strongest will in the world, I didn't know what I was going to say to him. He was someone that I looked up to, someone that is a brilliant logical thinker and would make sense of this situation, but as he answered the phone, I couldn't get my words out. I was no longer in control of my emotions, I was crying, and not making sense, I finally got it out, it still didn't make things any the easier, the call was short – that I can remember. The sheer enormity of this brought me to my knees in the hallway as I ended the call, the sick swirling inside my stomach taking my thoughts and my mind running wild with unimaginable dismay. As I lay with my head on the cold laminated floor in the hallway, I knew the unbearable awkward questions would come my way from family as to why this had happened, the terrible embarrassing things that I would not want to answer. Suddenly my phone was ringing, of course it was Natalie, her father having called her after speaking to me. The first question was about why I was going through her messages. Straight away I was feeling the guilt, had I done the wrong thing, was this my fault, my anxieties kicking me from every angle, laughing at my every move. Unable to speak a lot and feeling like I was the scared kid in the corner of the room I said not a lot, maybe I was wrong, maybe I had read the messages and interpreted them wrong, and possibly taken it all out of context. Later that evening she arrived home, more stern words were spoken, and that was that. The following day we woke as if nothing had happened. Weeks and then months went by, unable to forget, and place it out of my mind at what I had read that morning. I felt humiliated, embarrassed, but also guilty with it, I tried so hard to put it out of my mind, but the anxieties kept coming back, flooding my mind with the same questions, should I have done anything to prevent it, should I have even looked and discovered the other messages, round and round in my mind these thoughts would go, day after day. From that point our relationship grew further apart, I was trying to plaster things up. We tried to move our lives to a positive, we started to look for a house of our own to buy, we had of course lived in rented properties from when we first moved in together so maybe if we had somewhere that we could call our own it would make things just that little bit better, and yes it allowed us to focus on something for our future, which filled a lot of time in looking and viewing places to live, but deep down I was still having great difficulty dealing with what had gone on. When a situation is just thrust into your face unexpectedly, you have to address it there and then, you feel the pressure, then throw in the emotional side of the circumstances, and it suddenly becomes a hundred times harder. I have always been a type of person to shy away from disputes and confrontation, so when I was plunged into this god awful situation I just wanted things to go away as quickly as possible for the anguish that it was causing me. In spite of all these thoughts, to have our own place to call home was something that I truly thought would fix things, and allow me to forget, but how wrong I was, they just festered and manifested to the point where I wasn't able to take any more. By this time we had found a property, arranged a

105

mortgage, and had the deposit for the buy. I was really happy in the sense that we were actually going to have our own house, just so excited. I had run around tying up all the loose ends with the paperwork, paying the solicitors, and all the official documentation required for buying a house which we were hoping to be moving into just before Christmas 2016. I was scheduled to fly out to the Rio Paralympic Games for 18 days to work with the British Paralympic association, so I wanted to get things tied up as best I could before I flew out.

Spending the time away in Rio had allowed me some thinking space, and a couple of weeks after returning I made the decision that I couldn't carry on, and that I needed to break away. The timing was just terrible, we had just a matter of weeks until our completion date for the move, so many things had been put in place, but the unbearable thoughts of that morning back earlier in the year had just lay dormant in my mind until I had the space on my own to think clearly, if truth be told on a personal level I had both the time of my life out there, but also the worst, in the day my time was filled with helping others, and working with future athletes on their skills, to then at night I would often wake up crying in deep despair trying to find the answer to my emotional worries regarding my marriage, I was having to hide my nightly break outs from my roommate whom I was working with, leaving the room at unearthly hours to get to grips with myself with a swift walk along the sea front to clear my weary mind. Over the period of the 18 days I had come to the decision that I couldn't carry on with the marriage with what had happened, my only dreadful thought now was how I was going to break this one back home. It was something that once said, then there would be no going back. Could I live with the guilt and anguish of hurting someone I loved, telling her just as we were embarking on a new stage in our lives with the new house, but I knew deep down that even that was not going to fix my feelings I had towards what I had read in those messages, but which would be easier to live with, the fact that I would be living with the trepidation of them or the anguish of a separation, it was going to hurt whichever I chose, but obviously there must have been something amiss within our marriage for her to be distracted by somebody else's attention to her. In the weeks after we had spoken about separating and being still unable to bring myself to say to her that we should split up and that things were over between us the inevitable did come to fruition. Within a week or so she moved back in with her parents, things moved swiftly. I had to find somewhere to live that was fairly central to my current work, I helped with her moving all of her belongings back to her parents' house where 10 years earlier. I had helped her move out of and into our first place together. It was heart breaking, all these emotions just engulfing me, but I needed to stay strong, but all I in fact wanted to do was collapse and wish everything would just go away. Had I made the right decision, was this just another fuck up in a long line of mistakes that I had made throughout my life of wrong choices in years gone by. Half the time I was just in a simmering daze, unfocused of anything that I was doing, haunted at night by clocked figures of deep misery and trepidation. Months would pass never seeming to become any the easier. Thoughts of my love and timeless worship that I had for her, the moments that we shared at different times and locations around the world. The fun shared from years gone by now just left to haunt me while I slept, or while I tried to get on with my days. The days where I would head out on my bike to try and loose myself in training and gain some space would often end up in me crouched at the side of the road gasping for breath, feeling choked with emotion and bringing on the panic attacks, shrouding me with the fear of uncertainty as to the future. Running scared I would find myself making irrational choices leading to a catalogue of errors concerning my health. This was an area that I had been in before, self-harming and blaming myself for her actions that started this process, then obviously what came in the aftermath of the breakup.

Of course I take partial responsibility for it going wrong, if I look at everything that went on in our lives over that six years, it was too much pressure. We certainly neglected one another, but without realising it at the time, or maybe it just wasn't meant to be, I don't know, but it's happened, and you just have to pick up the pieces. It would be unfair of me to cast all the blame on to her. At the end of the day we still had feelings towards one another, even when the time came to separate. I was left pretty fucking cut up from where the whole break up had started from, the one single situation that sparked it off, and then to it ultimately ending the marriage. I was extremely fortunate. I had my small family unit who, while not fully understanding why we had split up or why I was starting to isolate myself from people, were still there if I needed anything. Looking at things now I probably should have spoken to some kind of professional for help in the respect of trying to deal with things. My anxieties took over, and I refused to talk to anyone, I thought that I could handle things on my own, but the bouts of depression were having a toll on me. My training was starting to suffer to the point where I would be out on a session and I would just have to stop, overwhelmed, I could not contain my emotions, this would happen several times a week without any sort of prior notice, I was trying to blame others, I was blaming myself , I was not dealing with things very well, I didn't know where to turn, all my life I have just dealt with things myself, but this was a whole new level of emotion. I kept telling myself that things would be OK in the end, I just didn't realise how long it would take. That was just over two years ago now. I still feel a bit lost; is this it, is this life, is this how it all works, you know when you have had something where you are of the mind set of believing that it's for keeps, and then something catastrophic happens, it leaves you wandering in a void of uncertainty for a long time.

People often ask me would I do anything different with my life generally, I point out that somethings you may never be able to change, or alter, you just have to keep getting up each time you are knocked down, and that doesn't matter how hard you are hit, you just have to keep coming back. Unfortunately at that particular point in my life it seemed as though there would be no coming back, I just couldn't see it, the end, not only had my self-esteem taken a battering, but also my own values of how I should deal with situations, such as questioning my own worth and not just to other people, but to yourself. For a long time, I believed that there was something wrong with me, for if someone that I was married to was taking an interest in somebody else, then I must have been failing somewhere in some aspect, or was I just not good enough, full stop. I started to self-harm as a release, a reprieve from the emotional pain. I would use it as a reset button, I would feel liberated in the moments after doing it, and that would allow me to survive another day and I didn't see that I was doing anything wrong. I had been here before concerning my racing career so I knew the whys and the wherefores, but I also knew the pitfalls. I needed to keep a lid on things and not let myself sink to the depths of substance abuse.

Would I change anything, yes, of course, I would have devoted more time into the marriage, something that now I have had chance to appreciate that I maybe wasn't doing, I would have had children and lots of them, but that's it, I think that boat has well and truly sailed. I'm not saying that having kids would have fixed our marriage, but had we had children a few years back it may have had a positive impact on our relationship in the respect of something that was a part of us, but I also think that we were obviously in the height of our sporting careers, so there was a lot of pressure there as well, I would still love to have some kids of my own, but I think now it is too late.

So what have I learnt along my journey of relationships, I've always chased or just drifted along with relationships in the past thinking they would work out or leaving it to the other person. That probably sounds a bit selfish, and you'd be absolutely right. In my younger days, and through my marriage, I was chasing something else, that was my racing career above everything else, and that's why relationships have taken a back seat. Now did I get it wrong, should my focus have been on other things like marriage and kids etc., did I get the balance wrong? Unfortunately it was timing, I look at it now and I wasn't ready for marriage at that time, that's why my focus was elsewhere, but now, yeah, maybe not marriage, but definitely some sort of companionship.

Would I say my marriage was a mistake? No, I'd say it has given me a very valuable lesson, a harsh one with all the shit that went with it, but sometimes things in life happen for a reason. I hate all them type of sayings and clichés, but quite often they have true meaning. Marriage is a 50/50 commitment and for the first few years I admit that I probably didn't work like that, then you just end up in that same rut. Before you know it the meaning of marriage, all the things that you had in mind at the start are now that far clouded over that you don't see any way back, and I'd say that was on both sides, then without realising it, you have drifted apart which then leaves you open to outside influences. That's not me pointing the finger, placing sole blame on Natalie, because we had something amazing at the start of our relationship, something that I will never forget. My time with her was adventurous to say the least, fun and laughs in the early years, but in the end for me I just didn't change a lot. I was still chasing the one passion that I had grown up on, the thing that was ingrained in me and gave me that intense thrill. I was just riding my bloody bike, still traveling the globe whenever I got the chance to. I was also enjoying a new role with the youth sport trust on the sky sports living for sport programme where I could inspire the youth of today. It wasn't that I didn't give a shit, I did. I was doing all the stuff that you do day-to-day, the chores of running a home and training to a full-time programme as well, but missing probably the important things, the components that really matter. I now know that, but obviously it's too late, but maybe I'll get another chance one day in some shape or form, who knows.

Hey look, life has its moments where you can be sat in a café or walking in the street, and you'll just stumble on someone that you instantaneously have a connection with. I'm still waiting I must say. I've been in hundreds, if not thousands, of cafés, and the only thing I've stumbled on is my own sodding feet, but that's not to say that the person hasn't been there. I've obviously just been sitting in the wrong seat or walking the wrong street, not that I walk the streets, that would be hideous beyond any stretch of the imagination, and that would be stretching my imagination, I can tell you.

I have heard people talk about deep heartache and how it made them feel and I never really understood what they meant, or to the severity that they would be describing it as, but I now know and can comprehend that exact feeling. Finished and at the end of things is all I can say, just one outside influence was on my mind, it was the only thing that was keeping me going because of the significance of why I was writing it and this chapter and its contents being one that I would have much rather not have been writing. At the end of the day it is only actually you that can drag the strength from somewhere to make those first positive steps forward. I have a track record of always getting up when knocked down, always finding a way through tough dark days even from such a young age. I was able to look at the situation, evaluate everything, try every angle and eventually climb over them barriers, but this time I felt well and truly beat, trampled on to the point that I felt that I was dying, that light at the end of the tunnel was fading.

After a few months went by I had to start thinking to myself that it's over, I suppose sometimes things just aren't meant to work out for whatever the reason. It's still hard to take and I will look back on that stage of my life and take the happy times and thoughts from it. I mean I could just let it eat me up inside, but that would be no good to anyone, least of all myself and I'm sure at some point my anxieties will again remind me from time to time that it was maybe something that I should have done something about at the time rather than letting it go.

Chapter 10
Chasing the Sweet Spot

I was never one into exercise or any sort of strenuous activity, well, apart from riding my bike round the streets where I lived. I think that may have been down to knowing that I couldn't run like every other kid, catch, or kick a ball in the same way. In fact anything that requires even just a little bit of skill or competitive edge I used to shy away from. In primary school I recall the teacher standing all the kids in my class in a circle as he stood in the middle with the ball. He would casually be throwing it at each child for the recipient to return it through a heading of the ball. I stood there wishing for myself to suddenly become transparent, to not be noticed in the circle of faces. I dreaded anything coming into contact with my head, or even anyone touching it unless I've had prior notice. It's a fear that haunts me, a constant reminder of the bang from the accident. As the ball travelled around from kid to kid, the dread was unbearable! I used to drop to the fall and pretend to do my shoelaces before the teacher had chance to select me. I would stay in that position deliberately doing and undoing my laces until such time that he would change the drill to something else. I don't know how I got away with it each time without him working out what I was up to. The tension deep in my stomach would knot so tight that I would often feel sick, leaving me unable to talk for some time after fearing of the consequences of being told off for not taking part with the rest of the class.

I wasn't a chubby youngster, pretty trim and stuff until I got to my middle teens, 13 or 14. I think every teenager goes through that stage at some point, just part of the development I suppose. When I very first started riding at the age of 14, I found it quite difficult, any sort of incline would just take it out of me. I would be left all red faced-with a massive sweat on my spotty brow. Once I had returned home I would just pig out on chocolate, sweets, and any other sugary hit that I could find in the house, not really reaping any gains, but just adding to my pepperoni pizza look. I suppose as a youngster you don't really have the foresight to understand the rigors that are needed to reap the rewards. Well, I wasn't, anyway, but things are different today. So I also got myself a paper round, it would be a morning round before school, a few lads at school had one, the pay was shit, well, based on today's standards, or even back then if I'm honest. It was a pound a day, pure slaving it, yeah; the round was two bags each morning, so there was me on my BMX at 5.30am seven days a week. I lasted about three weeks. One morning I was so pissed off with it that I just threw the two bags of the papers, leaflets and any other flyers that had been stuffed into the bags that morning by the shop owner off of a railway bridge. I then headed back home to my warm bed before going to school. It didn't take long before some of the folk that hadn't received their morning paper before 7 am were phoning the news agents moaning that they hadn't had their local rag. Needless to say that later that day the shop owner called around the house and was not in the best of moods shall we say. I candidly informed him that I'd got rid of the papers and that I didn't want the job no more. Another friend was part of a milk round that he helped out on before school that I fancied, but the local dairy was unable to offer anything at the time I asked. Probably a blessing in disguise, really, couldn't imagine trying to discard a milk float and its contents as no doubt it too would have become boring at some point. So it was back to the drawing board. I had a skateboard which I used to go out on a lot. Needless to say I would also fall a lot from trying one stupid sort of move that I would be trying to craft knowing full well that it was beyond my capabilities with not having the balance and coordination, quite often ending up in more pain from the falls. So all I really had was my racing bike. I eventually received a static training setup that I could use the road bike with, which made a huge difference as I could now train indoors when I felt like it. This then allowed me no excuse not to train. Needless to say I had the best of both worlds. Riding a bike gave me the freedom which I couldn't find or see that any other sport could offer. I was the only one in our school that was doing the sport, everybody else played football, or rugby, which for me, although not totally dismissing it, it was too much of a contact sport that I feared as I was so protective over my head and hitting it. The cycling seemed the safest thing for some strange reason, it sounds totally hideous I know now as I'm sat here thinking about it, but on the other hand surely I had suffered the worst that could actually happen on a bike, right? So anything from this point would be minor, well, that's my route of thought anyway.

I quickly developed myself into training and exercising on a regular basis, weekends and holidays were the better times as I had more time to spend on the bike. I had a kind of obsession with North Wales as well as some of the hills in the local area. From where we lived at the time it was only about 40 minutes down the road before any sort of climbing started. Pretty ideal actually as it gave enough time for a warmup. I used to set myself small challenges each week to ride certain climbs at a faster rate. Back in them days I had no computer mounted on the handlebars, no heart rate monitor, everything was done on feel, and feel alone, I would push myself until my heart was burning a hole in my chest cavity, my breathing became an almost thirst-like yearning, and the legs felt like anchors, I loved that feeling, a feeling of complete desperation for life, but also the knowing that each time that I felt like that, that I could possibly be making progress on my overall fitness. The majority of my rides would be done alone, that way I could be in my own world, I could hit out on a climb, or a sprint when I wanted to, I could ride for as long as I felt the need to with no distractions. I used to plan my routes from an old road map book that my dad had given to me from his then truck driving days. At first I would be looking for signs, and road numbers whilst I rode along from what I had seen in the book as I didn't really know my way around, the amount of times that I went off route, missing a sign, a turning in the road, or a landmark, but it was quite fun, I didn't really see it as getting lost, just more an adventure. Yeah, so it used to add time on to my rides, but it really didn't matter as I was free. Even now I stick to the same navigation process, I rarely use GPS which everyone kind of relies on these days. I don't even wish to use it if I'm completely honest, it doesn't excite me at all. I rely a lot on intuition, and all of my own senses, that goes for pretty much everything that I do in life. I think my biggest detour was around 35 miles which was in North Wales back in the winter of 2002. I was up around the back of Denbigh already having covered in the region of 55 miles. It was around 25 miles back home when I took a wrong turning and ended up down in Corwen. It was 3.30 in the afternoon with the sun setting and going dark. I knew the quickest way home would be to travel along the Wrexham bypass before it went completely dark. My idea was that with two lanes of traffic traveling in one direction at anything up to 60mph then I would benefit from free flowing air in the direction that I needed to travel, my idea payed off, and I travelled the 15 or so mile stretch of the A483 back to Chester at a fair lick. Pumped with desperation and adrenaline it's surprising what you can actually achieve when you visualise an opportunity. Another wonder ride that sticks out was towards the end of a mile munching seven-hour ride, again in North Wales. I was completely on my arse with nothing left in me, well, what I thought anyway as I dropped into the small town of Flint on the coast. I was around 10 or 12 miles from Chester when two articulated low loading lorries pulled out just ahead of me, fully loaded with heavy plant equipment. As the second of the lorries eased off to let some traffic through, I quickly passed it, I rapidly made my way up to the rear of the first low loader in order to grab a free tow. I didn't anticipate it lasting long as I knew there was a duel carriage way section coming up that bypassed around the Deeside industrial estate, by the time we had reached the start of the bypass the second low loader had caught up. So there I was sat in between these two articulate lorries, tucked in the best sweet spot that I have ever rode in, I was feeling the pull from the front being in the slip stream, and the air was now being pushed from behind me by the second, the feeling of the previous 90 miles from earlier in the day, and the 'on my arse' feeling that I had been going through 10 minutes earlier had totally dissipated. I now felt supreme, as the road started to elevate over a bridge I thought this is me fucked as we started to hit 50mph, my legs were spinning out in the 53x11 gearing that I had on, but no, the road crested the brow and down the other side we went, I had time to free wheel, and regain some kind of composure as I knew and could see the next hurdle of yet another elevated section of road, I also knew that there was a roundabout to configure first which would kill my pace. To get back up to speed after that was going to be the binding factor, make or break; however, it was going to work out. I would be well and truly finished when I got back home. I don't know what the two drivers must have been thinking… So as we exited the roundabout, I gave it everything to stay with the sweet spot which I succeeded at, but by the next roundabout I was spent 'and then some'. I think I crawled the rest of the way home on my hands and knees! I don't think that I have ever felt so bollocks and happy at the same time. I know you should never play with the traffic, and a lot of people would view it as dangerous, it wasn't so much the traffic that I was chasing, more the feeling that you get from riding in the sweet spot, the free flowing air that's sucking you along at pace when you're up close to your limit, and then still having the ability to push on hard holding it for however long it may last. I just really viewed it as an adrenaline rush. I have always kept myself at a distance with motor vehicles for if I ever needed to take evasive action at a spilt second's notice as you never know what a driver is going to do. I would never suggest doing it as it is dangerous. In more of a controlled environment it's OK, I mean that also still carries its dangers, but that tends to be more down to rider error. You look at say a road race, all the riders are on the limit, processing information, and making decisions at splits of a second whilst riding within millimetres of the next rider in front, and to the side of them, reaction time is everything in sport that you can only learn from doing it, you can't sit at a desk, and have someone lecture you, nor read it from a book. You got to get out there and put yourself in a situation that requires you to be extremely uncomfortable, but also have the ability to quick think. That's the best way of learning, getting into the field.

So as the seasons rolled on, I was becoming aware of different techniques in training, finding my ability to push on every different aspect, mentally and physically. New methods were being developed that I would hear about. I would either buy into it or not, I could see that some things would work for me and others not. I was always one to give it a go, but I was also one for if I knew something was working for me then why change it. A coached fucked up my then wife's swimming career as he was wanting to do things his way and wouldn't listen to her. Even months into his programme when things had gone backwards, he still wouldn't change. In a fit of desperation he was still pushing her his way and turned her from a world and Paralympic champion into a club swimmer within 12 months, just a complete bellend! I now hear he is working in somewhere like Thailand, probably running scuba diving trips to look for fossils! As an athlete you know your own body, what works best for it and not. Of course, you have to be openminded. When a new coach comes along they are going to have their way of doing things, but when you suddenly go from a champion to a chopper in a short space of time you have to question what has happened, you look at the changes and figure what's working and what's not. In her case he just kept changing the training like as quick as his underwear. It was a guessing game until not only he had messed her up physically, but the mental knock-on effect that she was feeling from her frustrations with him not listening, it just wrecked her career and shortened it by five years at least.

It wasn't until 2005 that my training took on some real shape, with the introduction of a new manager for the squad. Dave Mellor brought a wealth of knowledge and experience with him not just in a managerial sense, but also the aesthetics of how a professional training programme should look. For the next few years Dave tried to revamp the programme environment heading into the

Beijing Paralympic Games but seemed to be banging his head on a brick wall as to having the freedom to do things. Under Dave's guidance and Chris Furber as coach, I achieved world champion status, numerous world records, European championship titles and many more successful achievements. Training for me started to become like a drug from around the time that I started to work with Dave and Chris. I could see the drive in Dave, and the vision that he had towards the programme, little things that he would say to me or that I would overhear him casually chatting to another rider about would give me that lift if I was feeling down or not quite into training that day for whatever the reason, Dave seemed to have this infectious character that would lift even the lamest of folks. It was Dave that introduced me to training behind a motor bike through the coach Marshall Thomas, an absolutely lovely guy was Marshall, wouldn't say boo to a goose unless it shook a can of Lucozade up just before he opened it, or phoned him an excessive amount of times whilst he was abroad and left very short voice messages just to get on his nerves as it would cost him x amount to retrieve them which he would moan about each time. The only really scary thing about Marshall was the fact that whenever we did motorbike efforts with him, he would insist on turning around to chat at the same time that he was riding the motorbike which I must say freaked me out, this was also on the velodrome at about 40kmph so concentration was paramount…but I suppose that was Marshall, top fella!

Training and that need for the feeling of total exhaustion, that's what I loved, and still do crave a need for. Not so much the short track sprint drills, but the long endurance type of stuff, it's like if I don't get it I become really grumpy and pissed off, I don't think I will ever be able to let it go if I'm honest with you, must be in my DNA, my Dad raced when he was younger so that gene must have developed somewhere along the line. The motor pacing stuff I fell in love with, to sit behind a motor scooter for so many hours at a time really got my juices flowing, I think that is why I started training in Spain in the early part of the season each year as I was able to spend time just chasing my dad over all sorts of terrain for hours on end, I can't really explain the feeling, only that your rate is over what you would normally ride at, you don't have so much wind in your face so therefore mentally you feel that you can put more effort in, still maintain the speed, plus develop the skill of having to hold the back wheel for hours up and down climbs, in and out of corners. It's just another level that you wouldn't necessarily get if you trained completely on your own and unassisted. It's that feeling that I spoke about earlier of being at threshold, or just over, knowing that under normal circumstances you would be slowly drifting into the red of your capabilities, but then also having the adrenaline that is being fed to you in massive pools each time you feel the pull from the scooter. My dad had a place in the region of Murcia down on the south east cost of Spain, the roads in January and February in the local area would be completely empty of much traffic so we had the fruits of where ever we rode really. They were of top-quality asphalt as well, so super slick, low rolling resistance that just added to the addiction of motor paced sessions. I did a three-week camp out there in the August of 2011 just before the UCI para road worlds that took place in Copenhagen. I knew the training effect would be a lot different to say January or February as it was in the height of the summer. I recall the first few days it was very humid, very much out of the ordinary according to the locals, 40 degrees plus. For me I love training in a hot environments, it suits my body, and I don't suffer with the recovery as much as my muscles are a lot more relaxed which eases my spasms, so an almost perfect environment. That particular first week I could not stop sweating, the worst point was when I wasn't even on the bike, just sat in the chair doing nothing. I would be soaking wet, my body was like working over time, the more fluid and electrolytes that I put in, the more it just threw out like it was free, it's import to balance the fluid intake in very hot climates which I'm pretty good at doing, but this one week was just insane. I recall a trip to the local market on one evening, I was just stood completely still, just soaking wet, people were looking at me like I had just come out of the sea, I couldn't get away from it, it actually drove me mad as I looked around at other people, they didn't seem to have this issue of skin pissing water, I felt like a watering can! I seriously to this day don't know what was actually going on with my body in that first week, perhaps it was just a reaction to the very high humidity that only I was suffering from out of all the millions that were in Spain that week, that's how it felt, like I had been targeted by the Spanish heat police. Weeks two and three the weather settled; it was still in the high 30s to low 40s but was much more pleasant without the humidity. My training just went up a few notches as I was starting to feel really good. We were nailing each day as planned. My body weight dropped as I predicted with the strength and speed remaining! It's a calculation that you have to think of when training in any sort of hot environment as you don't want to lose any muscle mass as that is the thing that propels you forward. It's a fine balance again, packing in the proteins straight after your sessions are an essential part of the plan to rebuild and maintain them functioning muscles. Once I returned home I had a massive shock to the system with the temperature, I was having to wear extra clothes in bed, even a woolly hat just to keep warm, it was funny, but horrendous at the same time.

My next real step up in training came a few years later with the use of altitude, I had always wondered about trying it, but never really came across having access to such methods. Then after the 2012 Paralympic Games when I started switching my focus to endurance, targeting the road time trial events I found a sponsor to pay for a simulator with all the equipment for training as well as for sleep at altitude. Altitude training, what is it, I had to do a lot of searching on the effects, and which best methods to use to really capitalise on the benefits. Simulated altitude is where the barometric pressure is kept the same, but the oxygen content is reduced which also reduces the partial pressure of oxygen. This is simulated through the use of a mask-based hypoxicator system, or an altitude tent, so by spending several weeks at high altitude which is incorporated into a training block at preferably over 2400 metres (8000 ft.) above sea level, you can increase the mass of red blood cells, and haemoglobin in your system, thus increasing the capacity to carry oxygen to the muscles. Whether you are traveling to a competition, or just using it to increase your training load, you will have a higher concentration of red blood cells for around 10 to 14 days, giving you a competitive advantage. At sea level air is denser, and there are more molecules of gas per litre of air, regardless of altitude, air is composed of around 21% oxygen and 79% nitrogen, as altitude is increased the pressure exerted by these gases decreases, therefore there are fewer molecules per unit volume, this causes a decrease in partial pressures of gases in the body, which elicits a variety of physiological changes in the body that occur at high altitude. It's all very scientific, I could probably write a book about the stuff that I don't know about altitude using all the boffin jargon that is not in my vocabulary, but the basics are it makes you feel better, and go better for longer, but only last for a short period of time unfortunately.

For me this definitely had an impact on my training, and the longevity in which I am able to carry on my racing career by bettering myself through this method. In 2014, this became prominent as I started to move up the results board towards the podium places in the road events at international level, with a new coach (Richy Bott) that I sourced through the university of Chester, I was now able to tap into the physiological side of things. We were able to run protocols with both the altitude tent and the training mask during some low and high intensity sessions on the indoor rig (watt bike), I soon noticed the dramatic difference this was taking on my body, not only was my endurance levels showing a huge increase, but also my weight management and body composition were looking very positive. For a number of years, I had struggled with my body comp, in fact, most of my life I have had a battle with my body weight fluctuating like a yo-yo until I started with the altitude protocols. My weight management is more balanced now and this transferred over to my training and racing, but more importantly I noticed that mentally I was feeling much better. My overall health had taken on a whole new level, I felt good in training, could see the positives, that in turn contributed to my mind and thinking being much healthier which equated to better results when it came to racing. A completely new package had been discovered and I really wanted to push things on to see where it could take me. I absolutely fell in love with this training process, pushing myself at new levels, seeing the overall results just made for me wanting more of something that I hadn't seen before.

2015 was not a good season due to outside happenings, and situations that I struggled with that were unrelated to training, a down season really. We all get them, even the best have a dull season where you are doing all the training, but the racing results just don't happen for some reason or another, and you never really know why. In your mind you're doing everything you can do, then it becomes a vicious circle because you become frustrated and train even harder. The secret is to be able to identity what is going on and maybe take a step back, but most of us are driven and have the desire to win above everything else so quite often we don't see the tell-tale signs because they're obstructed by the bigger picture. Time and time again I have struggled with this, and time and time again I have said to myself to take a step back when it happens, but I never have, always beat myself up first… It's like we are designed with a self-destruct button!

2016 rolled, in and with all the equipment, complete access to coaches and lab time thanks to the university of Chester. I was going to podium at an international event. That was the target, the greater picture was to gain selection for the Rio Paralympic Games, but first I needed to show my worth, my first target was to win the British time trial championships which has always been a passion of mine from the start of my career. To win a jersey is everything in cycling, it's an honour and something that every cyclist dreams of. The training had gone really well all year, making progress right across the board, and with the added strength and conditioning exercises that the guys at the university of Chester introduced me to mixed in with all the altitude sessions, the all-round package was really showing. The next step was on to the World Cup in Bilbao in Northern Spain, I had worked my arse off and covered every aspect leaving no stone unturned. I had undergone regular physio and massage from a local therapist Stacey that I had used over the years as I needed to be in good shape, it was a guarantee that she would fix any issues that I had each time I needed it. I arrived in Spain in possibly the best shape that I have ever been in, and due to that, and all the hard work I walked away with a medal from the road time trial. It was a massive achievement from this newfound cocktail of training protocols that came from the altitude training, and everything else that we had covered. Unfortunately my results did not equate to making the team selection for the games that year, it was hard to take, as we had devoted so much effort over the previous couple of years to find a training method that suited me, one that would give guaranteed results, but that is the way it goes sometimes. We just have to look at the processes, and take all the valid points from it, and sift out the niggles as there were a few things that didn't quite fit. As we now go into the 2019 season I have big aspirations to try to qualify for a road world championships and then have one last hit out at making the Paralympic team for 2020 where I can hopefully see out my career with the ultimate prize, we have all the ingredients and training data now, and by pulling on all my experience of over 20 years I know that I would regret it if I didn't give it one last push to end my career just having really found this new technique of training. Well, new to myself; it's been around for a very long time, I just haven't been able to access it, and really get to grips on the understanding of such methods in the way that my body can adapt. I have been doing it for a few years now, and still I'm noticing gains in different areas that have never been visible before. There comes a point in every athlete's career when you know it's time to stop, that can range from suffering with a lot of injuries, or just a drop off in your ability to get results at events, or even just in training. It can be a daunting time especially if you become affected by injury as it's almost out of your hands should it get to that point, another power ending something that you hold a passion for, something that gets you up in the mornings despite the weather, the environment or how you actually feel. I look back right over the spread of my life, I feel so blessed to have been part of this sport, and to have stuck with it even through the darkest of times, as it's not only made me into the person that I am today, but also most probably kept my body from becoming a habitable grow bag for the disability that I have. I am certain for sure that being as active and fit as I have been right through my life has allowed me to keep my body moving and doing something that I love so much.

Chapter 11
Silent Suffering

11.50am, March 6th, 1990, the waft of cooked food drifted through the school corridors filling the classrooms on the lower floor with the scent of fried chips and freshly baked pies signalling that diner time is quickly approaching. Glancing around the room, you could easily sense that the half-asleep kids in the class that struggled to be aroused by words of encouragement from the teacher concerning the daily topic were now starting to wake, their thoughts directed at the hundred or so metre dash to be first in the queue for their daily fix of hydrogenated cuisine. Minutes later the competitors would start to gather by the door, pushing and shoving. You could sense that others in each classroom on the same floor were also of the same mindset, squeezed up against the doors like horses in stalls. The sound of the school bell like a gun being fired at the Olympic Games. Within a second the doors would be flung open, and the masses would spill into the corridors in desperation, the lessor characters would be pushed to one side, or squeezed at the doorways giving way to those that want it more, soon into the yard which would be saturated by now with others from the other buildings, all focused on the same destination; a small opening nestled between two walls, the finish line where the fruits for their efforts would be presented. Luckily, I wasn't part of this mortal combat. Me, I either went home for lunch, or went over to the local shops and to the chippy for diner with a more select group of diners…we would sit on a wall just around the corner from the school, stuffing our faces with curry and chips. It was a favourite, I can smell it now, just superb. Well, that's what I used to think as we passed the bag around. I didn't really have any concept back then of the importance of food and nutrition, we just used to eat anything and everything, but I suppose that went for a lot of things.

I clearly had something going on from an early age concerning my appearance. It all started in primary school where I developed some kind of flaky skin syndrome that would be confined to my scalp. That's OK, I hear you say, it's under the hair, nobody could see it, true. It didn't stop me from itching it. Once I started, I could not stop to the point where my head would bleed, but that still wouldn't stop the itching. The aftermath of that would be my school uniform looking like I had done a day's work at Quaker, again I don't know if this was stress related in some way, or connected to the trauma of my earlier accident, but it went on for quite a long time. The kids in my class would laugh at seeing me covered in dead skin, the name calling would then come off the back of that. Of course, I was having to use a special shampoo that had all the perfume characteristics of a public toilet, to which it was having no effect on what it was intended for. I had to persevere with it. Eventually this did subside just in time for the facial spots to appear in some sort of mass invasion, creating almost hourly visits to the bathroom mirror. My mum must have bought shares in Clearasil over the period of about three years. On top of all that came the dreaded visit to the dentist and the words from his mouth that every kid prays they will never hear, "Yes we can put a brace on there." Not just the one set though, top and bottom at the same time, so now I was having to deal with a face that resembles a pepperoni pizza, and a mouth that looked like some kind of electronics circuit board, how much tougher could things get! Not that I was a pin up in school or nothing like that, but to now have added to my not-so-popular outward looking reputation was the absolute tragedy of all tragedies! I started to become very conscious of my appearance at this point. Kids will be kids, and things used to be said, comments made that would hurt. At that age you don't necessarily have the foresight to see beyond that point, so therefore you let the situations get to you. You then start to believe some of the stuff that is aimed at you. I don't think I ever really commented on anyone's looks in school, whether that was because I didn't notice, or it just wasn't in me to insult another person. I used to blame myself for how I looked. I knew the shit that I used to consume was not the best, but it was all that I knew. Sugary drinks and food that were high in E numbers as they used to say, litres of fizzy drinks I would just guzzle down. This I can now see was probably adding to my skin conditions, a poor diet, terrible nutrition intake, and never enough water. It wasn't something that was in the media back then, things like child obesity wasn't even a word I don't think, mind you, nor were games consoles. Well, the Nintendo was just starting to lift off in this country, then the saga mega drive was the next thing to hit the market, but not to the point where you would stay in your bedroom 24/7, so yeah, we would eat all this shit and as you were hanging out with your friends about the estate, you would burn loads of energy off. Obviously, all this bad diet was a huge contributor to suffering with spots and flaky skin in my case. Around my middle teens I went through a stage where I went, shall we say, 'a bit plump' and quite noticeable! I was very active as in I would be out a lot, but I was obviously consuming more than I was burning, or my metabolism was at a stage of being lazy. I became quite conscious of it, my body appearance more so especially when it came to the PE lessons in school. I would shy away from getting changed in front of the other lads in the changing room, I wouldn't even think about having a shower after say a muddy session on the school field, a lot of the other lads were skinny to the point where they looked underfed, so the contrast was quite noticeable. The last thing I needed was to give them more ammunition to throw my way about my personal physique. I was by no means mega huge to the point where I would be exploding out of my school shirt, but I was certainly noticing that I was having to slacken the belt off more as time went by. This would play on my mind a lot. why was I like this, why wasn't I like everybody else? Life didn't seem fair, beating myself up inside my head. So, everyone at some stage in their teens goes through the whole hormones kicking in process in one way or another which can affect you in different ways. I look at it now and see it as a major process that can determine a lot of different aspects in your life, having worked with endless teenagers over the past six or seven years it has given me an even bigger understanding of it. 14 to 15, it's a pivotal point, it was at this stage that I decided that bike racing and sport was something that I wanted to do, not just on a weekend, or as a recreational activity, but it was something that I wanted to see how far that I could take myself. It started to change the way I thought about things; one of them things was my body comp, I knew from looking in the mirror that I was far from the athletic look that you could possibly get, but how could I change this, all I had ever known was eating anything and everything. Most of my energy came from chocolate bars and the like. Even when I first started riding, I would load my pockets with sausage rolls, pork pies and mars bars as that's all I knew. On some rides I was even carrying a bag on my back like I was on some sort of picnic outing, one ride I recall stopping at a shop, buying a mega pack of chocolate digestive biscuits and consuming the lot like they were going out of fashion before I rode home. For all the riding that I was doing I was still putting on weight. This was to become very frustrating because as time went by and although I was becoming fit, I was still struggling with my weight and physical look. Towards the end of my school years I had gained height, but still didn't like the way I looked as a rider, I had tried to limit the types of food that I would eat, but to no avail. The more I trained the more I wanted to eat. I would just be consuming junk food, anything that was quick, simple and easy to prepare. This was the battle for many years after my teens and into my early twenties. I was never one to pick up a piece of fruit, or have a huge appetite for vegetables even though my mother was a good cook, regularly cooking with a lot of vegetables, I just didn't really eat them, I found them bland and boring. If it wasn't fried or covered in a sauce then I didn't want to really eat it. This obsession with greasy fried food had obviously been a desire of mine since my early school days and sitting outside of that chippy. Once I became a full-time professional rider, things changed slightly, but I was still struggling with my body comp. In essence I had been left with the stubborn body fat that had been generated from my teens, but I now found myself in a high-level world of professional sport. I was competing at world level, seeing riders at six to eight percent body fat with huge amounts of definition. This was again having a negative impact on me mentally as I started to compare myself to how they looked. I viewed that as the way forward, the way I needed to be if I was to be competitive. I was burning vast amounts of energy in training and racing, then putting it back in the only way that I knew how. To change things would require a huge shift in not just food intake, but also my knowledge of what kind of foods were best to eat, basically re-educating myself. Very little was spoken about within the GB team in the early days, it was as though you were expected to know all of what you needed to do at that level, you were sort of just left to it... Things have changed so much now in their approach to these areas with them now having their own chef. After the disappointment of my 2004 season I took a huge in-depth look at how I could change my body composition, I didn't feel in control of my food as I was still living at home where most meals would be pre-arranged and prepared. I was still able to access all of the high sugar treats and the like from the cupboards which I had to build up a resilience, but found that I was giving in each time I passed the cupboard, or was in need of a small snack, or hit of sugar. In the years that followed I did a bit of my own research of small articles in magazines, watching sporting documentaries on the television, plus tapping into other riders as to their eating habits. They made it sound so simple of how to fuel yourself in training and competition, but again nothing really much about losing the extra kilos, it was as if they just assumed that you knew being a fellow athlete. It started to feel as though it was an unspoken subject that nobody wanted to breach upon for reasons unknown. It became quite frustrating as I wanted to lose some of the non-productive weight that I was carrying that I was embarrassed to talk about, but I also didn't want to come across as being uneducated to this. I could see everybody else around me looking very athletic to which I just felt that I wasn't there, or even going to get there in my current situation. In 2006, I moved out of home, and into a place with my then girlfriend. I was able to control my eating a little better but found that I was still opting for the sugary unhealthy foods. It was so hard to make that change; it was a constant battle. One day would go really well, then the next day I would just fill up on rubbish. It wasn't until the beginning of 2007 and after a health scare connected with my intake of energy drinks that I made a conscious effort to change my diet. Things started well, I laid off all of the sugary treats, drinks, and processed junk only to see that this was still having no effect on my body composition. I was becoming very disillusioned by the work that I was putting in which in turn brought on some anxieties that hadn't surfaced since I was a teenager. It left me feeling desperate and confused as I was not gaining the rewards that I wanted. This then led me to scouring the Internet for information, which then opened up a whole new world of diet pills. After much reading and feeling extremely apprehensive I opted for a more extreme way of changing things; I sourced diet pills and reduced my food intake dramatically. I hid this from everyone including my family, other athletes, and my coach at the time. This again was difficult as I didn't want anyone picking up on the fact that I wasn't eating much, and only really downing pills. I would train early in the mornings on an empty stomach which I wouldn't log in my training diary. When I did eat, it was almost snacking on very small amounts of food, making out that I was full if anyone was with me, or that I had just eaten and didn't feel like eating – all the excuses under the sun not to consume food. I would bloat my stomach with water first thing in the morning, and throughout the day in order not to get that feeling of hunger. I would feel dizzy at certain times of the day. I recall countless days where I wouldn't make the trip to the toilet as there was nothing to pass. How I was still managing to train I'm not too sure. I was, of course. targeting the team sprint that year, so my programme wasn't so much endurance riding, but more track-based sprint. My weight was starting to drop and after four months I could see in the mirror that it was having the desired effect that I had been looking for, but I wasn't done. Inside I still felt fat, even though the mirror was showing protruding bones and the like, I was still unhappy. I was at this point just a few weeks out from the world championships, but surprisingly in very good form, well for the one lap 20 second efforts that I had to do. My weight was at the lowest that it has ever been, tipping in at 57 kilos. I was worried slightly because the pressure on me to produce a gold medal at the world championships was immense. The difficult part was convincing myself that things would be OK, I was able to shift my now light weight frame from the start line quicker than I had ever done before, but I also knew that I was still struggling with dizziness and a lack of energy. I had to balance my intake of food in order to be at my performing best come the day of the race. I knew I didn't have the endurance, but as my effort was just around the 20-second mark then I knew I would be able to get away with it come the day, I just needed to be alert. Fortunately, I got away with things and we walked away with the title. In total I had lost about 8 kilos in body weight in a relatively short period of time, but what had this done to me mentally! Through that whole period, I had felt depressed and my anxieties took a massive hold on the way that I viewed myself. I hid it from family as much as in the respect that I was deliberately losing weight because of how I looked regardless of my training and performance. I don't know if things hadn't had gone well at the world championships what I would have felt, would I have blamed it on something other than me wanting to lose weight, or would I have just totally dismissed it and not given it a thought? It's hard to say. I suffered a lot over that period, I was so hungry at times and felt so ill at points, but I couldn't stop, I couldn't tell anybody through fear. I knew that I was doing wrong but was unable to stop. I had two or three things going on, my reflection being one thing, my mind another that was split in two; one part of its ego being stroked as to what I was seeing in the mirror, and then the other half in denial of what I was actually doing. In the following years up to the games in London in 2012 my food habits were fraught with anxieties, my weight and body composition unbalanced, but still allowing me to compete within the top three in the world in my races, but not delivering satisfaction within my own thoughts. My obsessions with food and the way that I looked that had stemmed from when I was at school had been a demon that was just not going to go quietly. I had to address this subject; it was something that I was unable to deal with alone as the demon would always have the last say. Post 2012 my outlook was to head on to the road and seek out some success on the world stage. The requirement to have more control in the respects that I had to eat for endurance rather than just sprint was a huge approach and change that I needed to undergo as I knew that I wouldn't get away with things like before as the events ranged from between 40 minutes to a few hours, so I needed to factor all of this in. My first big obstacle was how was I to lose the negative weight without compromising my power. I had spoken to a nutritionist that advised me on how I should be fuelling myself as the endurance athlete/rider that I was wanting to be. It wasn't long before I became deluded and engulfed in the whole diet pills, and the starving myself, this time though things would be harder, my training rides would start on an empty stomach, I would go for as long as I could without eating anything. I limited myself to one energy bar per ride in the hope that the weight would drop, and sure it did. I would find myself mid-training session wanting to stop and eat the grass at the side of the road as I was that hungry. I didn't know how, or where I heaved the energy from to complete any of the sessions that I did, as all I could think about was how I looked. This image was stuck in my mind of how I should, and needed to look, that was all that I was bothered about. At the end of each session I was so drained that the effort required to climb off the bike was unreal. My eyes couldn't focus, my arms and legs were like jelly, all I could think about was food, but that was the last thing I wanted. I would really limit my recovery intake to a small piece of chicken on half of a wrap with some bits of salad thrown in just to give it a little bulk. I lived on the same intake and variety of food for months without defaulting. Whenever we had a function, or be invited to a family meal it would really stress me out as I didn't want to eat, but knew I had to in order not to face awkward questions or looks as to why I wasn't eating. I just had to behave like it was a normal thing, each time I looked at a plate full of food it created a fear that the food was instantly going to pile on a load of weight onto me; this would make me angry inside, leave me feeling down until the next training session was over the day after. Then things would creep into my mind about the fact that I have failed or faulted at the diet. This would leave me in a state of not wanting to eat anything the following day in order to make up for the food that I had eaten. My mind was almost playing a game with me, allowing me to eat, and then punishing me for doing so. I started believing this processes that I would use it whenever we went out to eat, or to other people's houses. By me believing in the process then I wouldn't have the guilt of the questioning of myself to deal with. It became like the normal pattern that I was able to accept which made it easier. Over time my weight returned to the unhealthy 57 or 58 kilos which I was when I became a world champion in 2007, so in my mind I was settled and happy. It was hard to tell where things were because I was now competing on the road. Somehow, I had managed all of my competitions relatively well. What I didn't realise was, I was actually suffering with anorexia, my mind telling me that I was fat, by not eating, limiting the food that I would consume and then purging. I hating the way that I looked each time viewed myself in the mirror, seeing an image of me that was perhaps exaggerated to what I actually looked like, but my mind telling me otherwise, then acting upon what it had thought it had seen, but that in print would stay with me, it was something that had not just been brought about through my sport, but from way back in my school days when I was that plump 12 or 13-year-old struggling with that fear of getting undressed in the PE changing room in front of everybody else because I felt ugly and embarrassed at my body. As the years passed by my body comp stayed fairly stable, I was still hooked on the whole image thing of how I looked with my clothes off, I eventually found a number of a helpline that I called as I didn't feel comfortable speaking face to face with my doctor about things. I clearly had a problem but didn't feel that I could talk to anyone close to me about it either, I was embarrassed about the subject. I had only ever heard of girls and women suffering from it. It wasn't until I started to seek help that I learned that there are in fact many men that suffer with their appearance, food disorders and the like. I wouldn't have classed myself as having an eating disorder, and then once I deconstructed what I was actually doing in order to achieve the results that I was looking for. I was lucky in one respect that I was into sport, it was always in the back of my mind that I wanted to achieve, so it may be stopped me from going to the real extremities which could have had a huge negative impact on my career and perhaps even my demise.

Over the past three years my diet and nutrition has undergone the biggest change that I have ever been through. I now eat very healthily. You could, in fact, argue that it has gone to the other extreme, but I feel much better for it. I don't consume hardly any sugar apart from the odd pick and mix that I treat myself to. I don't drink fizzy drinks, nor eat processed foods, I blend a lot of nuts and seeds which I add to my daily routine. I am still very conscious of my carbs and proteins and the amounts that I consume, but I suppose that is the athlete background in me and I guess that will always be there, it's not such a bad thing really. I view food very differently now; I was in a sense educated the hard way, finding out through my faults and weaknesses that came from outside influences that created a fear like a self-destruct mechanism that I let fester and control my thoughts for many years. I would now urge anyone that is struggling with any sort of issues around food to seek help, it's nothing to fear, or be embarrassed about. I understand that a lot of the time people think that they can deal with things by themselves like I did, and occasionally still do, but it's important to not be alone, because that self-destruct mechanism will only become stronger until it's maybe too late. At the end of the day our human instinct is to live so don't suffer in silence.

Chapter 12
The Power of Inspiration

"Miss? Miss? I need some help, Miss?"

"What's wrong? what do you need help with?"

"I can't do this; I don't understand it…"

"Yes, you can, now get on with it quietly like everyone else!" "But, Miss?"

"Quiet!

Drifting along, uninspired by school and the teachers, the majority of the time I would often sit in class, disengage from the lesson hoping that someone would walk through the door, sit down next to me, and just offer a word of encouragement, but for me, it was just an elusive thought that would capture my vivid imagination most of the time. With the London 2012 Paralympics games done and dusted there was a lot of opportunities out there for inspirational speakers, after dinner speaking, and so on. I was never one to stand in front of a crowd of faces jabbering on, trying to make out that I'm clever in some way by cracking a joke, or searching the foggy corners of my cerebrum for a witty comment that I may have heard somebody else slip out at some point in my past. I struggled to read in school so the thought of trying to string words together on a stage would be a daunting thought. I did, however, end up being roped into delivering to companies and different organisations speaking about my journey as an athlete and how I had achieved in the world of sport. At one particular event that I was speaking at I was approached by a sky sports representative who asked if I would be willing to take my inspiring story into schools and deliver a package of activities for young people to engage in sporting activities nationwide.

At first, I was a little spooked by this. I had never thought of working within the education system at any level so to pitch myself right in the deep end of the school environment was a daunting feeling. As I was listening to this guy, I can remember thinking what I could possibly offer to young people. I ride a bike; I was a drop out at school and the words in my vocabulary you could jot down on one A4 sheet of paper. My school days had ebbed my self-esteem to an almost non-existent state 18 years earlier, so the thought of ever going back to that environment never made the bucket list. It took quite a while for me to pluck up the courage to call the number that I had been given a week earlier. I remember thinking to myself, *What am I actually doing?* This was outside my comfort zone, I didn't really like engaging with anyone that I didn't know, yet here I was dialling a phone number that was a gateway to just that. As I dialled the number, I could feel the anxieties questioning what I was doing. All I have ever known is riding, racing bikes and not a lot else. At first, I would have thoughts of not making the call, convincing myself that I was OK in doing what I do best and that I didn't need to add another string to my bow as they say. An athlete's career is not something that lasts forever, so with this in mind I started to have thoughts that this could be a new platform in my life, a new adventure. Reluctantly I made the call, it lasted for around 45 minutes. I was invited down to Loughborough university for an interview with the youth sport trust who the programme would be run by called 'Sky Sport Living for Sport', a free initiative for schools nationwide.

On the morning of the interview the nerves were jangling, I was feeling like I had taken a sleeping pill with a laxative. I just couldn't pull myself together. I was so in control of myself sat on the start line of the final of the team sprint at the Paralympic Games, yet this was a whole new level! I jumped in the car for the three-hour journey south. All the way there I had all sorts of thoughts running through my head; what if I froze, what if I suddenly lost my voice, what if my stomach decides it wants to empty itself? OMG! It was all going through my mind! Give me back my bike at a big international event any day, it's so much easier!

Suddenly I was pulling off at the junction for the university in Loughborough. It had been raining and a glumly morning for the whole drive down. This was it; the dark clouds had gathered; I was starting to feel the trepidation. After a bit of a faff finding the correct car park and a confrontation with the campus security guard after driving the opposite way down a one-way system adding to my tension, I arrived at the building. From what I can remember, as I hadn't been for interview since I left school I hadn't really prepared anything as I didn't know what I needed. It was more about my life story. To me it's all a bit dull, but obviously they had heard something that they liked. After 30 minutes of rabbiting on in front of three people that said nothing all the way through, it was pretty much over, they thanked me for coming and that they would be in touch. So that was it, back in the motor for the return journey. I had three hours to mull over what I had said and pull apart any seemingly daft comments that may have slipped from my yarning mouth.

I sort of put it to the back of my mind for the next few days then when I didn't hear anything, I assumed I hadn't been successful. Three weeks before Christmas, I was in the condiment's aisle in Tesco when the phone went. I quickly grappled for it from my pocket and answered it. A softly spoken Canadian voice was at the other end, "Is that Rik?"

"Yes."

"Oh, hi, it's Brett from the Youth Sport Trust." He was all apologetic that it had taken him so long to get back to me and would I be interested in joining the team. Still standing in the middle of the aisle, I couldn't believe what I was hearing. If I'm completely honest, with it being almost a month since the interview I wasn't expecting to hear anything. He then proceeded by saying would I mind going to a school on the following Monday as they needed someone to deliver a motivational talk. I was being thrown in at the deep end. I couldn't say no, so just had to go with it.

My first school was in Blackpool, I didn't know what to expect, I stood on the stage of an assembly in front of the whole school, almost 1000 kids. *Shit, I best not mess up*, is what I was saying behind my exterior shell that 2000 eyes were looking up at. I just ran my normal powerpoint and talk that I have delivered in the past to different companies which went down a storm. The feedback was awesome that I received. In the following weeks I was offered training to bring me up to speed on what I would be delivering to pupils as part of the sky sports programme, after which I was issued a list of schools nationwide that I would book in each week. I would not only deliver motivational talks as inspiration, but also practical sessions. I soon became aquatinted with my new role, the impact that it was having not just on the students that I would work with, but also my own development within the environment. Inspiring others just from what I had done in my life through a funded programme that was free to schools who signed up was a no-brainier really. I mean who wouldn't, there were athlete mentors all over the country on this programme going into schools every day doing the same thing as I was, the impact was off the scale.

My own self-esteem was growing with each visit, I was actually beginning to feel that I could see myself in this sort of setting in the future once I had finished with my cycling.

Again I look at my own childhood, going through school, we never had anything like this, all I wanted sat in the class in school was for someone to come sit next to me, to offer assistance to me with my work, or say something like, "You can do it" instead of just being ignored, or told that I wasn't quite good enough as my PE teacher once said on the run up to a inter school competition! I suppose I could look at it another way, as of the circumstances when I was in school and the way that I was treated, it actually made me into the person that I am today; the person that can now give back, that person that I was looking for all them years ago that I was wishing that would just come through the door to help me.

I have stood on the same path that many of the kids of today are standing on now, the difference is I now have the knowhow and the tools to assist them break down their barriers, chase their own dreams, and having been in that position of calling out and never being answered I can now hopefully be there to listen.

I have a huge passion for helping others, no matter who they are, or what challenges in life they may be having. So have I myself unknowingly missed opportunities because of my head injury which has resulted in me having to simplify the way that I do things. I asked myself this question over and over again for years until around a year ago when I was doing my support and motivation work in a school, then it dawned on me as to maybe why I was like this for so long. It was just a normal day, it was lunch time and I was stood waiting in a disorderly queue of kids, all eagerly waiting to supply their stomachs with their lunch off the menu. I was minding my own business when I sensed I was being watched, as I glanced to my right hand side, stood next to me, glaring up was a small boy with the biggest smile that I have ever seen, it's a smile that I will never forget. He did not blink, his eyes were fixed, there was an almost frozen moment in time at that point that I turned and looked down, he was tiny with a bag hung on his back that he himself could have actually fitted into had he wished to hide and go unnoticed. As he stood there in an almost mesmerised state, he proceeded to speak with a broad Wigan accent, "Reet." Obviously I knew exactly what he meant; working in a Wigan school you quickly have to get to grips with the local language, or else you're going to be out of your depth very quickly, and very unpopular especially in a school environment.

So he proceeded with his next words that he could not believe that he was stood next to an Olympian in his school dinner queue. The joy that he was expressing was infectious, as we exchange the standard small talk that you do whilst waiting for your lunch in a noisy school canteen, I could sense that his character portrayed similar characteristics of my own when I was around the age of 11 or 12. In the following days and weeks he was there at the same time every day, sparking up bits of random convos about this and that. At the next point he would call me from the opposite end of the corridors causing somewhat of a jovial atmosphere that would spread wherever he went. Whenever he would see me around the school, he would yell out with his signature call, "Reet". As time went by the short conversations would start to build a picture of this little fellas being, where he came from, how he happened to be at the school, quite a little celebrity with buckets of chat that I was able to relate to.

He too had been in a major accident a few years previous, he had gone through unimaginable challenges that most people would not be able to process let alone deal with, but here was this young lad that was just taking everything in his stride, like it was the normal pattern. I could hear things that he was saying that instantly I would recall from my own experiences, thoughts and processes, all with similar connections, yet this smile was fixed to his face each time we passed. After five months of work at the school I was asked if I could do some work with him as he seemed to be getting into a bit of bother within school for different reasons, only minor issues that had been identified, most of which could be distinguished with a little work as to make sure these little issues didn't develop into something bigger that could have a greater impact to his education in the following years.

After couple of sessions a week with one of the most chattiest 11-year-olds that anyone could ever meet, I could see that his processes in the way that he delivered himself could be misconstrued by others. I could immediately figure why he was doing the things that he was, as I myself had the same identical thinking processes as a child.

Let me try to explain a little on this. So let's say for your average person, everything that you learn, then grow up knowing starts unfiltered. As you mature, you start to file them into boxes of understanding when and where to use that information, throw in your logic and emotional thinking process, and you start to really develop your own character in the way that you deliver yourself at any given moment in front of any audience, and have the understanding what is, or

129

isn't appropriate. This is something that I myself have and do still struggle with which is brain injury related, as I have matured and due to the many different experiences that I have been part of then this itself has really helped in my understanding of my own neurological processes. So to now be working with this one boy that has been through a similar situation albeit with very different complexities and characteristics of its own, the basic foundation is pretty much the same. So I already had a head start as to the kind of processes that he was using or not using, it was a case of guiding him through this without telling him or instructing him of how things should be, but almost a gentle buffering to keep him on his own path. For instance, it would do him no good me telling him that this is the way that it should be done as that is then me installing my own thoughts on him, and that is not the way I work. I like the people that I work with to figure it out for themselves, then that way they not only comprehend the outcome of whatever it may be that they are trying to work out, but also they develop the learning of the processes of working things out on their own which is the most important and valuable asset that I can offer anyone that I work alongside. The power of processing a problem on your own is priceless beyond anything I know, that inner ability to be able to work out anything that is placed in front of you, to then feel that self-achievement is just incredible.

What I did not know at first was that this boy underneath the exterior shell of what looked and came across to others as utter confusion or unworkable ability, was that he was very clever academically which was even more interesting. His ability to take information in, store it and then tap into it when required was already there as a natural attribute. A maths lesson for instance, the speed process that he would show over his peers was outstanding. One lesson that I recall he actually corrected the teacher, pointing out that she had, in fact, made an incorrect calculation of a sum on the board which obviously she was highly embarrassed about. I just sat there with an inner smile, thinking there is something here that is being missed because others aren't seeing it.

I've sat there many times with people that I have worked with, just thinking that if only someone had been there when I was going through school, spent a little time to identify my needs, then I may have gone on to college or even university. Time is something that I love to give to people, because it's something that you can't get back, whether it be 10 minutes, an hour or a few hours. It is by far the best thing that you can give to anyone, and if you can give it for free then that has to be the ultimate gift when you're helping them to make their own lives richer in the sense of knowledge and self-worth.

Working with this one lad was unique as I understood his requirements if that is the right term to use. As the weeks went by I noticed that he was starting to change slightly, it was very slow, and when you're working with people who have sustained a head injury you have to allow allowances for the processing of any information that is going on, then allow time for that person to then realise that they can, in fact, start to do things differently without having a negative impact on their normal routine or pattern of doing things. Quite often with a brain injury dependant on where the brain has been impaired the person over time develops very easy routes and pathways within the brain of how they tackle things like day-to-day general learning patterns. I know for me I find it so hard to process stuff, even what would be the simplest of tasks to other people takes me some time to work out, sometimes I just can't headwork it because my pathways connect in a different way, that's where it can become very frustrating.

This frustration probably led to a lot of missed opportunities that could have opened doors. Unfortunately, I just ditched them to one side as I couldn't be bothered, I deemed it far too taxing on my brain, now being older I can see that. I also now know it is just a hurdle to get over. For me those opportunities have passed, but for people that I work with they are all for the taking as with this one lad where I could see that he already had the academic skills to absorb information and use it, he just needed to be guided in the direction to realise for himself that he is just as good as the next person, he just has to work that little bit harder to get there to reap the same rewards.

A chance meeting with someone that had also suffered with a brain injury and was just 11 years old, I was not only able to encourage him to do better and strive for greater things, but I was also able to identify that my own processes could still be worked on, which would allow me to still increase the pathways within my own brain to better myself. I was once told that one door leads to another, that you should never slam it shut as you never know what opportunities may become of opening one door to maybe go through another. If I take a look at the opportunities that I have had through doors opening as a result of some of my successes over the course of not just my racing career, but my life really and where some of them opportunities have taken me, the people that I have met along the way, and been introduced to, it's incredible to think that I started out where I did.

The power of inspiration, I was able to inspire others from my own adventures, discoveries and experience, yet still I don't really see that as I'm just me, the same person that I was when I was a kid, the same person that grew up on them streets and did what I did. So what's different, nothing. Your body ages, your brain develops and you figure a way in life that best suits you. Doors have opened along my journey to make my life richer in the sense of knowledge and experience. I'm not a materialistic type of person, just the simple things in life for me. I hope I have been able to pass on valuable content, open doors for other people along the way that I have either worked alongside or just connected with in some way, after all, that is why I enjoy what I do and why I go to great lengths to help people.

Working with young people gave me huge satisfaction knowing that I could be having a positive impact on their lives, most of the time I would visit a school just once for a full day, work with a group of youngsters from say a group of just 5 to a group of 20 or more, and in that one day I would notice the changes, the self-esteem and confidence grow in just a few hours for the students that I worked with. I used to sit in classrooms while some of the kids were getting on with small challenges that I had set them, quite often taking a moment to reflect on my own past of sitting in school. Thoughts would pop into my mind of my own struggles, that would then in turn put me right back in that little classroom where I sat as a kid with teachers ignoring me by not offering the quality time that I required, even if it were just five minutes. But now I'm changing lives. I find myself going from somebody that lacked ambition for doing anything else other than riding bikes, to now being full of aspiration towards helping others, and being able to offer what I craved for as a youngster.

I would receive letters from the schools after my visits saying how everyone enjoyed the day and would I go back, or I would receive invites to special award evenings where I would be asked to give out prizes and deliver talks to parents. The work grew year after year as more schools would sign up to the programme, thousands upon thousands of kids being inspired each year by athletes all over the country five days a week. My work on this particular programme lasted for almost six years until sky couldn't find the funding and the programme came to an end, so disheartening. When I think back to the countless lives that the programme itself had changed during its years, it was just invaluable to the young people of today's society. Not only had I the opportunity to deliver in schools, I also had the chance on more than one occasion to work and be part of the school games. It's almost a mini-Olympics, the whole setup in the way things are run is undeniably the best organised sporting event at youth level in this country to give the young people a real insight to what it would be should they go on to compete at the Olympic Games one day. I was there in a mentor role, so again sharing my experiences as well as running workshops to work on certain aspects or deliver challenges for the youngster to work out between themselves.

It was quite difficult to imagine that I was no longer going to be doing something that I had been invited to be part of, something that at first, I thought wasn't really my cup of tea. Then it gave me the perspective of making a difference to somebody else's path by offering my knowledge as I could see the difference that I was making to others' lives. It grew on me building my confidence to do more. I have had the privilege of meeting other amazing athlete mentors and hearing their own stories. I have met some just amazing young people along the way, and I have developed within myself to strive forward with my own ambitions.

Towards the end of this programme in 2016, I was asked if I would like to go and work out at the Rio 2016 Paralympic Games for the British Paralympic Association on a mentoring programme that again was aimed at the future up and coming athletes that had been identified for their potential in their given sports. Of course, this work was exactly what I was used to so I excepted, it was for the whole duration of the games. So it would be two weeks in Rio with a small cohort of new athletes that were possibly going to be on the radar come Tokyo 2020. On the flip side I was going to be at a game that I wasn't going to be competing at, but working, so the opposite side of the fence as to say. I literally went from working at the school games in Loughborough on the Sunday to flying out to Rio on the Tuesday, it was a quick turn around and with the work being very similar it was fairly easy to cross over what I had been doing. I had my own perspective of what was to be an amazing experience out in Rio. I was apprehensive about how I would feel once I was there, and not competing. Six weeks earlier I had competed at the final round of the road world cup series out in Spain where my performance was good enough to step on to the podium. Obviously I was in pretty good shape, but it did not cut any ice in making the selection for the Great Britain team for the Games, so this being in the back of my mind I would always be thinking 'what if', so when it actually came to the event that I wanted to target I was of course going to be watching for the results coming in just to see who did what.

Once the first group of potential athletes arrived for the programme, we got straight to work introducing them to the ways of a professional athlete, how you need to approach a major event, and basically the whole performance lifestyle that is required at this level to perform to your absolute best. Things like what you should be doing to make sure you're looking after your wellbeing, getting your rest, making sure you're fuelling correctly, and all the finer details that are going to add to the overall performance. It can be hard for some first-time Olympic or Paralympic Games athletes at their first games, not knowing what to expect. I remember my first in Beijing, it was very different to what I expected, you can obviously control the controllable elements, it's quite often the things you didn't expect or don't even envisage that can affect you by having a negative impact on what is to be the performance of a life time. For myself back in 2008 in Beijing, it was the volume of athletes from all over the world. I was used to travelling and doing the daily things that involved being away from home, competing as I had been doing now for a number of years. I had never been in a situation of hundreds of athletes in a confined area, it was horrible, in fact I just wanted out most days, going to the food hall each day was driven by anxiety and shear dread. It probably sounds ridiculous, but there were days when I would lose my temper and quite often felt like I just wanted to lash out at people as of the volume of people pushing and shoving in the queues for food, it was like some people had never eaten before, then you have athletes in wheelchairs running over your toes just bowling their way through like they had the right, it was a right mix and mash at times. After my competition I found myself in a situation where I very nearly hit somebody as they shoved me in the back in the queue, how I held back I do not know even today. After that incident and a cumulative of other things I went straight to the team GB office and asked to be put on the next plane out as I could not stand it any longer, and the very next morning I was on my way home. It was hard because I wanted to experience some of the sights, I knew that if I was to end up in a situation in the food hall again it could have been serious, so I took control and got myself out as it was the best thing to do.

In the weeks that followed returning home I struggled a great deal to get grips with normal life, I found things were far too much effort to deal with, I was trying to soak up the atmosphere of returning home, all the different engagements we were to be invited to, but it was as though something was missing. People talk about anti-climaxes from certain situations, I never really understood what they meant by that until after the Beijing games, my days felt empty as though there was nothing to aim for. From the outside I probably gave out the persona that things were all good when in fact I was struggling. Representing your country at any level is an honour, but this was a new height, and then a new low, but as a typical athlete, I waved it away only to be troubled by it for the following six months before I could actually deal with the whole process, I used this experience and valued it to take me forward and on to the London games in 2012 which proved to be invaluable.

During the Rio mentoring programme that I was part of I was able to share and put across my experiences of how to deal with things such as the above. Hopefully this knowledge along with other work that we did would allow these new young athletes to gain the knowledge to hopefully carry them forward to help them achieve in the future at major competitions. I knew I had a wealth of knowledge to pass on to people, more so athletes because I had been there and done it, made the mistakes, and also been through the processes to learn from them.

I learnt a lot in Rio, not just about the programme I was part of or about the country itself and the culture, but I learnt a lot about myself as a person. The past couple of years hadn't been the easiest, obviously I had lost my funding from British cycling which led me to some soul-searching places. I also had to find my own way to carry on with my racing career through self-funding which alone was a huge task to undertake, there were times in Rio when I was able to reflect, but also to visualise what I wanted for my future, I knew I needed to take some time out from the sport because it had gotten to the point in the last twelve months where I was just banging my head on a brick wall. I knew I couldn't go on for the next few years with the same outcome. Things also hadn't been going well with my marriage for the past I don't know how long but things had sort of been brought to a head a little earlier in 2016, so I had those thoughts also contributing to everything else that I was mulling over. I met and worked with a great set of people in Rio as well, which was making me feel different about myself in a much better way.

I suppose I look at this period of my life now realising that not only was I to inspire others in their lives, but in having the time to reflect on my own life I was able to be inspired to change my life and my destination.

Chapter 13
Safely Guarded

With most things in life, we want to find something that we enjoy, something that we gain satisfaction from. For most of my life I have been looking for a passion, something to pull me from my bed in the morning with the excitement that I am going to be doing something worthwhile. A feeling that will make a difference! Racing bikes as a professional athlete gave me this buzz for many years even on the roughest of days, in recent years it was noticeable that I was starting to obtain that same sensation for assisting youngsters with their lives. With this new platform starting to take shape, the visualisation of my future work helping the youth of today realise their full potential was taking shape. It was full steam ahead putting all my experience of not just my mind and ability of a champion athlete, but also my entire self-drives along with my determination that I had developed as a young child going through the chaos of those days and weeks that followed my accident. I can now share that knowledge with others so as they too can develop and reach new heights in their own lives, to not just have the tools to succeed, but also the ability to overcome any testing times of their own, allowing them to build their own self-esteem, plus to give them the know-how to push on their levels of achievement even in the most turbulent of times that life can throw at youngsters these days. Life is about resilience, having the capabilities to muster on, no matter of the conditions, you have to take the rough with the smooth. I see this chapter as the pinnacle of everything that I have ever done, values that I believe in, everything I have fought for, taken on in my life, and have succeeded at and that has shaped me into the person that I am. I have dealt with everything that has been placed in front of me, I chose never to ask for help as I needed to feel the extremities in order to experience the full brunt of whatever I had to face and the hidden consequences.

The month was May 2017, I had just returned from Belgium where I had been competing at a World Cup event which was to be my last international cycling event as I had planned to take a year out of the sport to not only concentrate on my new venture, but also to sort out some health issues with my legs that had been troubling me for the past few years. With the Tokyo 2020 Paralympic Games being three years away, I still had sights on competing there, so felt this was the right time to address these issues as well as having a bit of kick back time.

Two days after returning home my first assignment was to mentor a young lad that was a school refuser which required me picking him up in the mornings to spend a few hours with him to prepare him for re-integration back into school at some point. This is classed as outreach work so it can be quite challenging; the complex situation required careful thinking, a strategy had to be put in place as to keep this lad interested as I was to be working with him five days a week. Nevertheless, I embraced the work. The work was very bespoke to the boy's lifestyle where each day was very different to the last. In the first few weeks it was about building up the understanding of what he was about, passing on my expectations of the work we were going to do in order to prepare for school. Quite often you have to step back and take a look at the greater picture. I had to analyse his whole setting, living conditions, and his needs as not only someone I wanted to get back into school, but also someone that needed life direction. The reality of the situation is that there is a brick wall in front of you which can only be taken down brick by brick. It's an unknowing number of hours' work, a lengthy process, and there is no quick fix for this as a young person's life is in your hands. All the different agencies through to social workers that had been involved in this boy's life were unable to make a difference, then I turned up, just another face to add to a string of people that have been in and out of his life over the years. The difference here was that I was brought in to be there every day for him, five days a week that lasted for almost 12 months.

May 21st, 9.50am, a windy but dry morning as I drove the 23 miles to the address that I had been given only 24 hours earlier due to a security purpose that I was made fully aware of before I signed to say that I would carry out the work. My mind focused on the processes that I needed to go through on my first engagement. I was a little anxious as I pulled up in the street of northern 1930s built terraced houses, the pavement lined with blue recycling bins, plastic bags and the odd carton blowing aimlessly in the street having obviously fallen from some of the overflowing bins. A feel of slight eeriness filled my thoughts as I turned the engine off. Not a soul around as I made my way to the front door of the address that I had wrote down on a scrap piece of paper. After five minutes of knocking at this door a scrawny figure appeared, half-clothed as though he had just risen from his sleep.

"Yeah? What du want?" spoke this small, but full of cockiness boy.

"Is your mother there?" I replied.

"No," he said, in an abrupt manner. After explaining who I was, he swiftly informed me that she was out all day and may be in the following morning if I wanted to call around then. With no direct number to call to try to locate the mother I was left with no choice than to return the very next day. With a slight deflated feeling I left. The next morning, I returned, eventually after knocking for some time I was invited into the home. At this particular point, any of the outreach work that I do it's good to build a background on the person that you're working with that will enable you to construct the right sort of path for the individual. Our first session I had decided that we would just have a chat at the local library, a quiet setting, but on arrival the librarian informed me that we weren't allowed in as he had been banned from the premises for past troubles even with myself as his support worker. This was to be the same wherever we went to in this small village where he lived. The reputation of this 11-year-old would limit us on a daily basis. We did eventually found a café that he had also been banned from which after some convincing with the owner we did actually have somewhere to go each day for our sessions. I found that he was very fidgety, struggled to sit still for more than five minutes, lacked respect, but I think that was more down to the fact that he had no comprehension of what respect was at that point in his life. With the pandemonium that this boy had going on I needed to probe into things via his social worker, which when addressed and armed with all the information I really was dealing with one of many extreme cases in the UK, but all I could see was this young life, shouting to get out and be heard. Other workers that the boy had worked with in the past had all walked away, unable to make a difference, or for whatever reason they had given for not wanting to work with him. I recall three weeks in and feeling completely flummoxed by the whole thing, but I had to be true to my inner self, my values! I believed in this lad, this lost person. I was not going to be one in a long line of people just to walk away. He needed a foundation, and that's what we needed to build. That decision I made to stand by him through his difficulties and be there come what may change his life. What a huge difference this was, you learn to take the rough with the smooth, and it wasn't all smooth, but eventually he could see that I was reliable. I was different and I didn't judge him. There were days when I had to really push him, to motivate him just to get up in the mornings. His little life and the turmoil that was going on around him no child should ever have to face. The hard exterior he'd presented to me on that first day at his front door was no longer there, I could see the characteristics of a young vibrant person busting out the more time I spent with him, the happy smiley face that had been held at bay by his anxieties at the chaos the surrounded him on the day-to-day basis was now being ebbed away by more enjoyable times. He learnt from all the experiences and chats that we had, even on the most difficult of days when I would be sat leaning against his bedroom door as he lay motionless on the floor from the night before, often starring at the ceiling, eyes wide open. It was as though I could see everything that he was thinking as he projected his sight in the misty darkened room. I watched him grow over that time from a small, hard-to-engage, wayward 11-year-old, to a more than capable 12-year-old that had matured and developed to a point of having the ability to make the right choices, the trouble-free decisions that will hopefully lead him to great achievements. The funding was limited, only being allocated for school term times; this made things difficult to which an issue arose during the summer period as he was involved in a police matter that put our work backwards after him being involved in the taking of a vehicle. He was enrolled on a youth-offenders register for his actions which was a huge blow to the work that we had done. What became quite noticeable was the lack of enthusiasm from the social worker that was allocated for him, I was aware that he was sleeping on the floor in a room with no furniture, he was left to fend for himself regarding food, equally his hygiene was very poor. When I asked the social worker to address this pointing out his living conditions, the response I received was very unhelpful to say the least. A lot of days were very difficult as it was, I'd call around to the house and find he either wasn't there or he was still asleep from having been up the night before roaming the streets with friends. With the parents also being involved with social care I really thought the social services would have stepped up a little more as this 11-year-old boy was definitely not being safeguarded against as of the conditions that he was living in. The parents were doing all that they could but were receiving very little assistance. It was difficult for me to take a back seat while I could see this going on. Still being new to this area of working on a one-to-one with students, I needed to leave the more intricate side of things to the social services. As time went on I could see that things weren't changing, I could see why he would stay out all night, or be around at a friend's house, I mean I wouldn't want to sleep on a floor at any age.

After five months and numerous meetings we secured a school placing for him, this was to be a challenging time, it was a PRU (a pupil referral unit), and as he had spent over a year out of mainstream schooling it was a daunting thought. A whole new environment, a new routine which tested his metal, his hard exterior shell as he was being placed in a hostile environment that he would probably react to, my work was to step up to the plate, not just in making sure he started to absorb the education side of things, but also to make sure he stayed safe and untroubled. It was to be the most testing time for him. Education-wise I could see he was very clever from sitting in the classroom with him. However, I could sense that he wasn't happy with the environment. Each day there was some incident evolving other students to the point that one morning we both were actually asked to leave as the other students were feeling very angry towards the boy that I was working with, even the staff feared that there may be a reprisal. Sounds bizarre, I know, but it was very real. The kids there would quite often carry knives, each morning they would be searched as they arrived in their small gangs. So we were escorted from the premises via the back door on this one morning, I feared for my own safety that morning for sure, but my initial thoughts were of my student and making sure he was safe.

After that day the schooling was hit and miss, he didn't want to go back, but who could blame him. I was there for him to which we had talks with social workers about how we could deal with this, but no one seemed to have any definitive answers or suggestions as to the next move. I feel that the social services network had not only let him down, but also myself. It was undeniably a difficult situation from every aspect, but from a safeguarding point for the health and mental wellbeing of this young person it was disgusting. I was left dumbfounded by the lack of action from the social services by the time that my contract came to an end. I know from my point that I had done everything that I was able to do without crossing any boundaries, which was extremely difficult to do, as I could see that the situation required going into a lot deeper in order to keep this lad on track as I not only felt, but could also see that this young person was reaching out, to not be answered, he could be lost in the not-so-distant future which will be a great travesty to the effort that he had put in during my time with him.

Chapter 14
It Hurts

In the October of 2017, an opportunity came along to work in the afternoons at a school to assist with a student's engagement. Initially it was just for one student in year 11; the school had exhausted all their options leaving them somewhat struggling to find fresh ideas that would allow the student to stay on the right flight path to deliver them to, and through their GCSE exams, so I was sourced through the external agency that I was registered with to engage with them based on my good reputation, results and expertise in this field.

The days were long, but the rewards were amazing. I was up in the morning, driving over to the one student that was my outreach work, then into the school environment in the afternoons. The school assignment was very different to that of the home mentoring that I was involved in, it required a little more planning as of the situation, again quite bespoke. At first, I was working with two students, the complexities were very sensitive that I can't really go into. From my point of view, I was hearing their frustrations that they had going on. The majority of my time was spent assisting them in class with their studies as directed by the school. I was having some success with breaking down the barriers that these students had which would show in their behaviour and attitude, this would then show in a positive way producing better academic results with less behavioural traits. In turn this would lead the students to being of much better health and wellbeing as they would be enjoying the fruits of their labour.

After a short while things were gathering momentum and starting to grow, my mornings would be based over towards East Lancashire where I would still be working with the young student as normal, then over to the Wigan area for the afternoon to carry out the school-based work. The final few months with the young outreach student were quite difficult, we had reached the point that they wasn't going into school, they were in a much better place in themselves than when I first started working with them, but it really concerned me as to what would happen once my work ended. I was a little apprehensive as well as upset at the fact that when my work did end that the student hadn't managed to be placed into a mainstream school; the social services were doing very little to have something in place for them leaving them with very little support. My work ended in the March of 2018 to which the student said that their life had been filled, that they could see the positive changes that they had made due to which they no longer struggled with their anxieties at the severity that they had been doing.

As my other work continued in the afternoons within the school environment, momentum was gathering with the success that I was having with the few students that I was currently working alongside. It was February time, just two weeks before the half-term break when a student approached me asking if she could work with me. FA or several weeks now she had been stopping me in the school corridors, asking the same question. I had of course been saying to her in previous weeks that with the limited time that I had in the afternoons, my capacity with the other students that I was working with that I would struggled to fit any quality time in for her, but I could see as she stood there with the bitter February wind blowing a few lonely leaves past her feet that she presented a look of an outcast. Expressing the look of wanting to discuss something with me I felt that I should at my very least have a chat with her. I had put her off countless times in previous weeks so I felt dutybound that I needed to plan some time for her. I scheduled for the Wednesday afternoon during her last lesson where we were able to meet for a chat to discuss if I could in fact be of any assistance.

The Wednesday afternoon arrived where we met up in the school library, she seemed very quiet at first as she sat there. Nervousness clouded her eyes, fidgeting with the frayed sleeves on her jumper as though they were her only stress relief tool from time gone by, the low self-esteem shouting out via her body language of shrunken shoulders and head slightly tilting forwards as though not to make eye contact. The discussion was lengthy. Quite clearly there were a conglomeration of things that she was facing academically, as well as life in general. I sat listening, all the time trying to navigate all of her concerns. I agreed to plan some time into my schedule to assist her with different ways that she could apply herself, offer some coping mechanisms that could help towards her self-esteem. With every student I come across you always need an open mind; not every student is the same, nor do they react straight away as there is more than often an underlying factor to their circumstances. I always place this first when working with any individual.

So the Friday afternoon came for our session. As per normal, I was running slightly late from another class. I arrived at the classroom where we had agreed I would meet her. I was greeted by her teacher that informed me that she had been taken by one of the deputy heads. On first hearing this I had a sinking feeling that something was wrong! I swiftly headed over to a part of the school where she was most likely to have been taken. In the midst of some confusion from other staff members about her whereabouts, it became clear very quickly that things weren't good. I hastily tried to find out some information regarding her to which I was informed that she was in a great deal of bother! She was to be expelled for possession of alcohol on the school premises. I was gutted, why had this happened, why now just as we had planned the first session. Confused and anxious as I started to question myself, *Perhaps I should have listened to her weeks earlier, was this my fault that she found herself in this awful situation?*

In the current climate of the school environment regarding mental health and wellbeing I am conscious that it is imperative that every child that I come across receives my full attention, but I was now questioning myself if I had missed something weeks earlier when she first approached me asking for help. I didn't get to speak to her that afternoon. I was later informed that she had been issued a five-day expulsion, with the possibility of permanent expulsion on her return to school for a meeting. This would take the time scale to two weeks with the half-term to take.

On her return the school had agreed on a very tight, very non-forgiving plan that she was to stick to without any slip ups. I was asked to work alongside her each day as her mentor. I knew with my experience as well as skill set that I could in fact assist in turning her ability around. The pressure was enormous for her, the type of character that she was portraying was that of a stubborn teenager that would do what she wanted, when she wanted, without a care for the consequences, but this is the environment that I thrive in. My passion, everything I believe in, motivating and inspiring young people to very high levels is not something that you learn from a textbook, nor is it something that is developed over night, it's years and years of experiences of your own, countless hours of beating on your own craft that actually teaches you self-discipline, self-motivation, self-drive, with the ability to deliver in the harshest of environments.

Like with every other student that I work with, the first session is key, it consists of just 2 elements, breaking down barriers and developing an understanding of how we can maximise the result! Simple! For this I use the interaction of playing with a tennis ball and chatting at the same time, no rocket science, just plain old human interaction. A lot of kids these days are quite often suffocated by games consoles, or feel too attached to their phones, the so-called reality world which can bring a lot of dysfunctional characteristics which can develop mental health issues. Mental health now has never been so huge in the public eye, with myself I have suffered with it, you shy away from talking about it as you view it as a sign of weakness, especially as a man, a world class athlete that I was, but it's imperative that we talk about these things!

After throwing this tennis ball backwards and forwards to each other where it was pointed out that I was pretty bad, but not letting her witty comments deter me, I switched the game up to goal scoring/saving where lo and behold! her weakness was identified. This session works every time, the ice breaker, just amazing in its own right.

In the first week I could see that my hardest task would be to keep her in check, not let her slope off. The determination within her character mixed with a desire to achieve was astonishing, she would try to hide that quality by putting up a hard-exterior shell. I'll admit now, this girl was as hard as nails, nothing would faze her. A huge fan and player of rugby she would think nothing of barging her way through people, her dainty physique would struggle to throw a shadow to the ground beneath her, yet she would show no fear in tackling someone of three times her size, and harsh environmental conditions would often pass by unregistered on her radar. I identified that she had attributes that if channelled in the correct manner, anything would be possible. Being so used to just doing what she wanted at any given moment, her biggest challenge was to recognise this for herself. After about two weeks I noticed that she was making that conscious effort to correct herself in the seconds before she would normally fly off the handle, which gave me the sense that she was buying into the programme designed to channel her thoughts towards the result that we had set.

The school had issued her with a report card for around six to eight weeks to which any negative feedback would carry some harsh sanctions. I think when she first viewed, this it left her feeling quite defeated as she knew the character that was driving her prior to this point would be the dominant force in carving out her path. We worked absolutely tirelessly each day, I can remember having to work her out very quickly in order that I could read a situation before it had time to fester, kicking off her snappy personality meant that she could turn quicker than a blue bottle. If I could be one step ahead of her game then it would defuse any situation before it had chance to grow.

I obviously had the other students that I was working with in the same school with different challenges with continued changes in dynamics for myself. The whole set up was quite complex requiring diversity from my point of view, I found myself dashing from one class to another making sure that I was overseeing everything that I had set myself. What you need to keep in mind when working with a vast range of students of all ages is the fact that things do change so you have to allow for that, not be too rigid, keep flexibility within the margins. I have to reiterate that as it's an integral part of the successful work if you want the student to achieve their goal in a realistic environment that they are happy with. At the end of the day the student is placed in the centre with everything else constructed around them, for them, in order to allow them full responsibility and ownership of their own destiny.

As time went on things had been working really well with regards to her progress. The fact that she had not received any bad feedback against her name the school placed her on a planner check system in replace of the report card that was initially actioned.

We eventually reached the point where she started opening up about different aspects of her life, and other issues that she was struggling with. This is the normal procedure with a lot of youngsters that support workers spend a lot of time with, they build up that almost security blanket effect where they become comfortable speaking about their concerns which is so much better than locking things away where they can fester leading to undesirable thoughts to which then can create a situation that could lead to sometimes fatal outcomes as is documented all of the time now through the press as well as other social media platforms about child mental health and wellbeing. We have just recently witnessed the government announcement that there needs to be big changes in the way we tackle this ongoing problem within not only schools, but colleges too.

With reports from the likes of young minds in UK and various organisations, all hitting the headlines about under pressure teaching staff, schools having to hit targets that had been set, the shift in schooling now has the approach of hitting figures and statistics rather than actual student centred wellbeing, which should really be the catalyst that's put before any figure or box ticking procedure, which following that would produce results both academically and in general wellbeing. We now find ourselves in a climate of having to find a route of reversing the damage that has developed over time which is going to take years; one, to develop the strategic plan, and two, to try to undo an awful lot of the damage that has left so many youngsters along with university students bearing the scars of years gone by.

Obviously, prevention is far better than cure. In this particular case now we don't have much of a choice, you could actually run this under the banner of safeguarding, because in essence we would be safeguarding the complete future of not only our students, but also our education system for perhaps other nations to take knowledge from, to then develop even further, in a sense two or three heads are better than one as they say. If we were to lead the way on this subject, then that would in turn make us a very attractive nation when it comes to education.

Well into my placing at this particular school I had around 12 students that I was working alongside, all with very different challenges going on which had to be neutered in very different ways depending on the complexity of their particular needs. The initial reason why I was at the school was for this one student, this was difficult work in itself to start with, but once I got to grips and developed the right strategy with them, it became relatively easy to manage, hence why I was farmed out to work with these other students. Of course, there were times when I had to put the hours in with this one student, but I think because of their maturity, the understanding of myself and the engagement with the students' small group of school peers. Then they were able to buy into the whole situation that their GCSE exams were paramount to the next phase of their life after school, I was constantly reminding them the school is a very small part of their life, but all so a very important component that will stand them in a good position for whatever they want to do in life. My own schooling when I look back at it now wasn't so much about the results that I didn't achieve, but the experiences that I had. That may sound like a quote from someone that is uneducated and doesn't have a care, but truth be told what other options did I have at the time, my brain was already working overtime to deal with my physical impairment, so my attention span for anything else took a back seat. It was only as I approached my late 30s that I became able to take in information like education and process it. It's quite exciting for me, my ability to learn now is at a new level, I'm actually enjoying taxing my brain with the likes of the English language and math, chemistry and physics. I think because I have had a very practical hands-on sporting career, that I can relate back to that where physics and chemistry is concerned, also maths as I was dealing with calculations in physics when having to drag the absolute most out of my body and any equipment I would use to propel my bike forward.

With the English side of things, I'm always looking to correct myself whenever I write letters to make sure I'm using the correct terminology so as not to get things misconstrued. Years ago, I wouldn't have even had the capacity to even think in this manner whereas now it just seems to be at every opportunity that I am looking to better myself in this department. A lot of people would probably turn around, say it's too late, why even bother. The thing is, you are never too late for bettering yourself, nor increasing your own riches within, you don't have to be a rocket scientist in your 20s or 30s. Education these days seems to be rushed through and its hammered into you that if you don't do this and this by the time you leave school at 16 then your future is in jeopardy. Yes, I understand some of that, but I think that's mostly to do with schools needing to hit targets. Everyone is different, everyone has their own pace, everyone will achieve in their way and what they want to achieve. Ofsted has a huge part to play in all of this; they are demanding results from schools, running them like they are on the stock market, and not taking into account the pressure the teachers are then put under which filters down to the students in a very negative way, kids are being worked into the ground these days, it's almost bordering on slave labour in a way. The circumstances that children are taught in can have a big impact on their mental health. If the current climate and approach in schools doesn't change then we are set for a huge break down in the not-so-distant future.

I am extremely happy to say that the particular student that I was initially brought in for did stick at things, they sat all their mocks and went on to sit the GCSE exams, I think now they are doing an apprenticeship in their chosen field. I feel so proud of them and to have been just a small component in their journey, I wish them all the best for the future.

Meanwhile the female student was having her ups and downs; I was starting to hear her inner screams, could feel the chaos that was hounding her, she was responding to her academic work which was great, I just felt there was something deeper. Often appearing out of nowhere, I'd see her stood looking ever so lost, almost frail like in the middle of the corridor, or nestled in a stairwell at lunch time grasping a half-eaten sandwich which seemed to be her only comfort. During the changeover of lessons in the midst of the hustle and bustle of the narrow corridors I would see her pushing her way through to come looking for me throughout the different sections of the school with an almost fearful look of insurmountable anguish laying behind her eyes, standing in the doorways trying to catch my attention, quite often appearing without notice, softly speaking as if not to interrupt me if I was with another student. She was clearly in some sort of distress though often masking it with a witty remark hoping that I may not notice. In the coming days I spotted some marks on the top of her wrist that carried the characteristics of a blade. She never openly spoke about these marks to me at first, though she kept making reference to them by rolling her sleeve as well as making somewhat of a fuss with her other hand. I could sense there was more going on in her life than she was speaking about, it was only a matter of time before she would open up. I reported what I had seen to the relevant people; though without her actually disclosing any information to me, I felt helpless. It was like each time we had a session she was wanted me to ask, to make the first remark towards what I could see as she kept making jesters towards the marks which were distinguished in their appearance. In the coming weeks she would speak of the way other people would be treating her, speak of click bait that she would be receiving that were extremely nasty, a form of bullying. Although she didn't speak of the marks on her wrist, she was making reference to sharp objects, at some points she would collect pencil sharpeners, scissors and paper clips to which I found myself removing from her possession that she had taken, quite vocal in the fact that she had taken them for a reason, so through fear of her doing harm I was able to retrieve these back from her. All these incidents were documented, yet there was no forward plan made for her via an outside agency like CAMHS or other means. I started to feel a great sense of responsibility towards her, nobody else seemed to be doing anything. I would find myself checking in on her at every opportunity during the school day, picking up the pieces, reassuring her that all was good, that we were going in the right direction to our goal. I couldn't understand the sudden tilt as why she seemed to be becoming more isolated from others, and then the unthinkable happened. It was lunch time, I had just finished my dinner and was on my way to get ready for another session when she stopped me in the school yard; we had a discussion about our session that was planned for later in the afternoon, when all of a sudden she swung out with her right arm catching me on my upper left arm, instantly she froze in moment of turmoil, I pulled my arm in to my side to absorb the blow.

Her eyes beginning to well up on realising what she had just done, the fear growing in her voice as she spoke, "I'm sorry, I didn't mean it. Shit! What have I done!"

I had to think extremely quickly what to do; all I could think about was the work that we had done, the fragile state that she was in and the consequences of this now situation. I must have asked myself a hundred questions in the space of just a few seconds reaching the conclusion that it would be of no benefit to her if I was to report the incident, she would have surely been excluded which could have led to a catalogue of undesirable thoughts in her mind which may have led to the unthinkable. For sure it will have been caught on cctv as the school yard had more cameras than David Bailey so if anything was brought to my attention I would have just had to weather it in some way, but my foremost thought was that her wellbeing and mental state came first in all of this. She knew that she had done wrong in her actions which prompted me to do right by her. We had been doing really well up to this point with things, she seemed somehow to be letting things get to her a lot due to outside pressures. I'm unsure of any school policy and the consequences of a student hitting a member of staff, but I was sure that given her background that she would have been removed from the school so at the end of the day what would that have served. From working with a student before that was in a situation where he wasn't in school and the difficulties that he was facing, then for her to end up in circumstances where she had no school to attend, surely that would have been the wrong action for me to take. For weeks I thought about that decision that I had made, waking me in the middle of the night, filling my mind with trepidation, I figured it would only be a matter of time before the cctv footage would be stumbled upon, leaving her fate to succumb to the powers of the education policies. I carried on working every angle to inspire her into believing in herself. As we approached the midway point

I still felt that things still weren't right with her wellbeing, there seemed to be no forthcoming action from the school around counselling as I thought that maybe the school would have brought in CAMHS at some point after I reported the self-harming marks that I had seen. She had made huge leaps forward from almost becoming permanently excluded from the school, she really had worked hard at things academically, the incident in the school yard we had moved on from. I sensed that she was becoming a little frustrated, and during one of our sessions she rolled her left sleeve up and revealed that she had self-harmed. It was a massive blow, she was clearly upset as she was stood in front of me, her arm blood covered, weeping from the many abrasions that she had inflicted upon herself, that look of fear masked her eyes once again.

"It hurts," she said, "it really hurts when my jumper sleeve snags," the pain showing on her face.

"Come on," I said, "let's go and clean that up. We'll get you a dressing put on it."

"I don't want to see anyone," she replied.

"I have a duty of care," I said. "It will be OK, there's nothing to worry about." I took her to one of the heads where she showed her arm. I felt as though I was unable to do anything, I wanted to help, but felt restricted; I could also see in the months prior that she hadn't received any help from others, just myself was there each day, helping her through her schooling, reading, writing and applying herself to her work, keeping her on track, but obviously there was something deeper, a more underlying issue that was causing her to harm herself. She said that influences such as bullying was causing her to feel bad about herself, which in turn she would want to hurt herself and to take her own life, I could relate to what she was saying, having been through the process of self-harming myself which can be a very dark and lonely place.

I decided to ask her to start reading to me, to direct her focus on to something fresh, it was something that she hadn't really done before, to read out to someone, and I thought from a self-esteem point of thinking it would give her new dynamics, so we selected a few different books with the help of the school librarian. At first she would read in spits and spats, unconfident and feeling slightly embarrassed as anyone would really, reading out aloud… Seeing that she was outside of her comfort zone and clearly struggling to express herself, I said to her to give me the book and that I would read to her. Now I'm not known for being a reader at all, I have read only one book in my life time as it takes me that long that I get to the point where I actually lose the story line due to my stuttering of words when reading, but I thought if she heard me read it will most certainly want her to take the book back as me reading can be quite painful to hear. Even when reading to myself my own brain tells me to shut up! I can say it did the trick, just half a page down, she ripped the book from my grasp catching me by surprise, then carried on reading herself, from that point she never looked back, completing three books in just five weeks, and winning a prize from the school librarian based on the amount of words read by any student in her year for a set period of time. I was so proud of her for sticking at it, accomplishing something that she was so uncomfortable about doing when we first started. What came from this one exercise was quite astonishing, she was suddenly starting to shine, she was starting to feel better within herself. I would ask about the self-harming and how she was feeling now, she pointed out that the marks on her arm were disappearing and that she wasn't going to do it again as she felt in more control of her emotions towards this. The determination was evident, for I could see the remarkable difference in her attitude a few weeks on from that low point, shoulders would no longer be shrunken, her head would be positively lifted with her eyes focused on whatever task was placed in front of her. Other teachers would comment on how she was a changed person, the look of despair that had coated her face over the previous months had vanished to be replaced by the look of courage and curiosity to develop, empower and grow into a much stronger person.

As the last few weeks ticked by, we completed the final book as I wanted her to achieve this before I left. For myself I could see the huge steps that she had made from when we first started to where we were the day I left. I think for her she had found something in her life that was maybe just the things that she was needing, the thing that was to just give her that confidence to push her self-esteem on. Obviously now I was leaving, did she have the strength to carry on, to still keep applying herself, to recognise her challenges and know what to do to not let them fester. I was sure she now had the tools, and know how or what to do if things got to a point, or if she was to say become stuck in a situation whereas she was unable to work out how to deal with it. After all, we had spent four to five months, day in day out working on these things, through dark days and touching on subjects that were very traumatic for her. There was a poignant moment in the last week I worked with her that summed up the whole time in quite a surreal way, during a chemistry lesson as she was fidgeting and swinging around on her stool. It suddenly slipped from under her. Within that precise moment I reached out grabbing her wrist to avoid the inevitable, the look on her face as she was suspended between the table and the floor was that of fear and relief that she had been saved, quite fitting I thought. I have every confidence now that she will go on to achieve great things to which she can look back and think yeah, that was a time that changed me for the better or that was a difficult period in my life, but because I listen or I took an opportunity to which I was able to change things to make it better. Like in the earlier chapters, it's about inspiring others, we all have qualities that will inspire someone in some way to do something that will change their life, like myself writing this book at this time, I was inspired by someone and I've done it because of that one person, so thank you to that person.

Chapter 15
LIT

I have always wanted to feel loved by someone outside of my small family circle, but to be honest I never got that feeling at all from anyone. I like to be treated the way that I treat people, but I have always felt that I am the one that's putting more in, maybe I'm putting too much into people or expecting too much back, have I set my standards too high? These are the things I have asked myself over and over again for years. My family showed my brother and I a lot of love when we were younger so I think that has set the bar, it's installed in us how to treat someone that you have so much care for. I see that when I spend time with my brother's small family, that's what I crave. Obviously I spent a lot of time in my sporting career away from home so my passion and love was probably suppressed slightly as I was chasing something that I had deep inside of me that I couldn't let go, that was probably a contributing factor to my marriage ending, but at the time you don't see it, or you do, and just keep saying it will be OK when really it isn't and won't. With friends it's slightly different, but still I was never around much to have what I would call a solid friend. I still keep in touch with James who was my best friend in school, again I wouldn't say we were close, but is that because we very hardly see each other. I mean in school we would see each other five days a week, then again maybe over the weekend, so that connection was always there. Once we left school, we would see each other though it would be more hit and miss at staggered times as we were carving very different career paths resulting in us soon drifting apart as we became older. When we do see each other, which is once in a few years the feeling towards one another is still the same. The conversation isn't an awkward thing to get going at all, so when we look at it like that maybe we should try to see more of each other, maybe I should put the effort in, after all we were never really apart in school. Once we left school it all changed, right through my late teens and into my 20s I didn't really bother with each other. I was too fully concentrated on my training and racing to have the time to even go out, always saying no to people, I wanted to reach the top of my sports, perhaps looking at it now I did restrict myself a horrendous amount. I lived like a monk, everything I did was for my goals, my racing and fuck everyone, but where did that mentality come from, because I am a deeply caring person with a lot of love to give, yet I let the other side of me take over a massive proportion of my life. Was it something from a child, was it my accident that caused me to be like that, to have the single-minded determination, was it anger from being treated like shit in school, ignored, always looked down at from other kids and teachers, because I don't think it was normal, well, normal as normal can be. For years I was like this, my time seemed to be filled with racing, training and travelling, so I suppose my mind was occupied with all that. I became almost like a loner, aloof and was finding it hard to let people in. Then Natalie came along, things changed, well for a little while, then I slipped back into that routine in a way, but now I had someone that was also filling another part of my life so there was like a pull in another direction, not as strong as the other. It was really hard to try and find that balance with stuff, as I had gone for so many years blocking people out, I suppose it was a massive adjustment that I didn't want to undertake. Don't get me wrong, I treated her as any man should, but I was never there in the sense of when she really wanted me there, my selfishness took over towards my sport because that was the automatic reaction that I had only ever known, that adjustment for me wasn't made easier, I just aired to what I knew was a safe and comfortable situation. Instead of embracing that new occasion I would find myself fighting it because I thought it would impact on what I was trying to achieve, when in fact I wasn't looking beyond my handlebars. There was only Natalie in my life, there was still no friend as such, I had the people I trained with that were my associates, but no one I would call a true friend, we were all of similar mindset being athletes. As any athlete will tell you they have two sides to their personality, the competitive 'I want to win at any cost' side, then their normal human being side, and then there was me. I was just a 'twat' and couldn't switch off because it had been going on for so long inside of me, closing people out at all cost.

Even when I was married I struggled to adjust as I couldn't let go of what I had known from such a young age, we had a circle of so-called friends, but I wouldn't say I trusted any one of them like you're meant to with true friends. They were always talking about the others in the group when they weren't around, that set me thinking that they must be talking about us when we are not around, so that trust was never built up as I wouldn't let myself be part of that talking about people that you say are your friends, but will talk about them when they're not there. It's strange, when my marriage did end not one of them once made contact to see how things were, not on a personal level anyway so I was right to keep my distance in listening to my inner self all along. That still doesn't make things any easier though. I mean I wasn't consciously looking for a solid friend, but it would have been nice to have someone. I had Natalie, they always say that your wife is also your best friend, but things didn't work so it obviously wasn't meant to be. Once all and done I resigned myself to the fact that it's just me; I can rely on me, I trust myself, I can look after myself, so do I need anyone? If there is anyone they will find me by whatever means there are.

I'm not the superstitious type nor do I believe in love at first sight, what I do believe in is that things happen for a reason, and that maybe something else that happens way in the future, my path will cross with somebody else's, that may only be for a brief time, but it will bring purpose and meaning in some way, shape or form. You will know if it will be something that you want to invest in short term, or a longer, more meaningful adventure, you will know just by the way it settles you. I'm guessing you have to trust your own inner feelings. Being very tuned into yourself will make the decision almost a natural way of thinking without any negative thoughts, like it's non-negotiable as there isn't anything to negotiate, so in other words it is meant to be. I don't put that down to superstition though some people probably would argue the case, but meeting by chance where your path crosses with somebody else's is like a one in however million chance there is on the planet. When I look at my past now I sometimes analyse the chance meetings that I have had, my biggest one was obviously the wife, or the driver of the car that knocked me down you could say. In no way am I suggesting that they have similarities being that of a disaster but make up your own mind. So I looked at all those people that I have met, and what the purpose was, the outcomes and the duration of the happenings and if I have learnt or taken anything of value away from it, my answer would be yes, whether it be a positive or a negative. I have definitely gained in experience of knowledge but may have lost in respect of friendship or companionship which I do miss in a way.

Another aspect of the way that I look at the whole of my life is that I feel as though I have drifted along a little bit doing this and doing that, never really aiming at anything that long-term. Maybe that is just me being critical of myself, I have never thought about retirement like most people do, I haven't anything in place for say a retirement fund, I have never looked at saying what age to pitch myself saying yes that's a point that I want to finish work and kick back. I have always taken things day by day. I'm just having fun now, kicking back whenever it takes my fancy, not really thinking about the future. Now whether that is down to my head injury, and not really having that sort of expanse or planning mechanism, I don't know, that's not me being lazy or having a CBA attitude, but I just feel from a planning point of view when it comes to the likes of things like finances and situations that I associate as adult responsibilities then I just tend to steer away. Don't get me wrong I'm responsible, but we all have to admit that stuff like bills and shitty paperwork we would rather avoid as it just more so than often brings instant anxious feeling within me. At the end of the day it's crap that you don't need in life, so I just don't engage with it at all. I can't remember the last time I opened a letter that came through the front door, I just tend to pick them up and file them on the side unless it's a handwritten envelope, or it's something that looks unusual, or something that I am expecting. I mean why do the utility companies need to send you paperwork when you have a direct debit set up, their getting paid each month so what's the deal, the same with all the other stuff that arrives. I mean why would you want to even engage in stuff like that? Life is full of enough stressful situations anyway, no one wants to add even more pandemonium to it. I wouldn't call that irresponsible, I just don't see the importance, I don't know, is it important, maybe subconsciously my anxieties are playing a part by ignoring mail then it removes that trigger of feeling more anxious which then leads to feeling depressed, or am I just putting off the inevitable in risking an even bigger problem later on. Am I afraid to make that step in taking charge of things, I have always shied away from situations that seem too complex, or is it just a case that I am lacking confidence in myself in certain areas of my life. I mean it even has me thinking that am I even meant to be here, did I pull through my accident by fluke, am I now living a life with no purpose nor direction just wandering lost, unconnected, or did my accident do more damage to my brain than was originally discovered, was something missed that would now explain all the mental limitations that I feel, did it lock certain chambers within my cerebral which has hindered my development into adulthood? I really do think there is something amiss.

To some people I live my life without a care in the world, without being responsible. Some have even said that I am selfish, but I suppose that's their opinion. The true fact is yes to a certain extent, but I value things very differently, I am not a materialistic person, possessions don't really mean a lot to me. living life, having a good time, not worrying is how I try to live life. I value the riches I have inside of me, the things that sing a tune that no one else hears.

From around the age of four, well when I first started primary school we connect with people, other kids etc., mine was a lad called James, James Green. He was a quiet lad just like myself, he lived out away from the housing estates in a cottage that was isolated on a main road behind a petrol station. We quickly became friends in school, we would see each other on the weekends, mostly I would go to his house for some reason, I think it was better as he had fields with lots of open land around where he lived which was great to just go a play. Boys being boys, we would get up to all sorts, playing with toys cars in our younger days on some muddy lumpy ground at the side of his dad's warehouse as his dad owned a removals firm so there was plenty of space. The fields that ran alongside their property would belong to the farm that was around a mile away. Each year obviously farmers rotate their fields so growing crops one year then cattle the next, after we had done playing we would sneak into the field amongst the crops pulling freshly grown potatoes from the ground, ripe corn on the cob, or whatever was growing in the fields at that time of year, we would then take our haul back to the house where his mother would cook our lunch. Just absolutely amazing taste would come from the food as only an hour or so earlier it was still in the ground, or still on the branch where it had been growing. OK so technically you could say it was stealing, but at eight or nine years old it was just stuff that was growing in the ground to us. Every weekend I used to look forward to the delights of that fresh produce. Obviously during the winter months those fields would be empty or maybe filled with cattle of some sort.

These moments in my life were wonderful times; me being me, doing stuff that I would just do without thinking about it, the innocent acts that would bring joy, happiness and harmless to some extent, those times that I could very easily go back to now and would feel completely comfortable with as those moments were like my escape, my most pleasurable times of fun and adventure. Obviously, we grew up a little, or did we? We would still venture into the fields, with often more daring thoughts as to what we could get up to. About a mile and a half in the opposite direction to where the farm was situated, just beyond a wooded area of trees, there was a garden centre, well, more the back end of a garden centre that the public didn't have access to, so an area where all the working machinery etc. would be kept and stored. It took us a while, but after numerous attempts to cross the fields navigating a small stream that divided the garden centre from the wooded area we did in fact gain entry over barbed wire fencing that snagged us a few times. The stuff that lay before us we had no idea of how it worked. After sneaking around making sure not to be seen we eventually found an item that is used by farmers in fields to scare birds which works on pressure building up, and then releasing a rather loud bang from this funnelled tube that stuck out at around 3ft in length of the front of this thing. Of course, my eyes lit up on seeing this. I suggested that we take it as we could have some fun. Now James being James, well, he was very innocent. Me, I was more street wise so it took quite a bit of convincing to get him to play ball. We started to shift this thing that was really heavy and with it being connected to a gas bottle of some sort it made it quite difficult to manoeuvre, we eventually managed to drag this thing to the fence where we had entered through a hole that we had made earlier. Unfortunately, we could not go any further as it would have meant lifting this piece of machinery which was far too heavy. At this point we had been spotted by an angry worker who was making his way over to us. James started to panic and was trying to scramble through the barbed wire fence while I was laughing. I couldn't stop and on doing this I then spotted a value release switch on this machine. Well, I just had to turn it, after just a few seconds *BANG!* this thing went off. I shit you not, I was definitely stood far too close to it, defining I would say sprung to mind, still I was laughing as this thing charged itself again. *BANG!* once more. I suddenly realised that this thing was going to keep going off catching the attention of more people 'cause this thing was pointing directly at the guy running towards us who had suddenly stop running, possibly as he was feeling the full projection of the defining bang. I was still laughing even when I was getting caught by the barbed wire fence on my hands, the adrenaline was flowing at a fast rate as we scrambled into the wooded area.

"Keep running," James shouted, I was still in a state of laughter struggling to keep up. We soon were in safe distance of James's home, we could still hear the bangs going off in the distance, but we could just not stop laughing about it.

As we got into our teens we moved more to playing with actual cars, yeah real working cars, his dad had a massive yard which we would drive these two old rusty cars around. We would practice our mechanical skills that we didn't have on these two motors, we would patch up the bodywork with newspaper then spray over it. Yeah, it was shit, but we enjoyed it. We successfully changed the driveshaft on one of the cars but blew up the other one whist driving it around the yard. I noticed smoke coming from underneath the bonnet as we sped around the yard, the smoke soon became flames which engulfed the front end fairly quickly which left the car goosed and undrivable. We still had the one car with the new driveshaft, well until James ran it side on into his dad's forklift truck which left a lasting lurching effect on the handling of the car. James blamed his dad for that accident as he actually appeared at the window of the house which distracted us leaving James unable to swerve out of the way of the stationary forklift truck.

In between spending time with what was to be my best friend I also used to knock around with two brothers that lived a few doors down from our house, we would just hang in the street and stuff, play on our bikes just doing what all kids did back then. One frightening moment sticks out in my mind that I have never been able to forget was that of one afternoon in the summertime. It was warm as I remember wearing shorts, our street was situated around the corner from the high school which back then the public could just use the school playing fields as well as most of the grounds to play on during the day or evening when the school was closed. One afternoon we were playing in and around the buildings when we came across a young lad on his own, probably 14 or 15 years of age. He seems to be hanging around where we were playing when he sort of jumped out, exposing himself whilst muttering some words that I can't remember. He was quite a nasty looking character. Being scared, we just ran off. I am unsure of whether we actually informed anyone, I was nine at the time. It wasn't until a couple of years when I started at high school that I came across the same person, he was in year 11. I can remember avoiding him whenever I would see him in the corridor, petrified every time he appeared at the thought of him recognising me. I don't really know what to make of that particular situation, it's stuck in my mind. Thankfully nothing ever came of it, but on reflection it was frightening at the time, then discovering that he attended the same high school was something that really freaked me out. For the whole of year seven it would play on my mind and cause anxious feelings of uncertainty until he left the school.

As I drifted through my teens there were a small group of lads from the estate where we lived, I think on today's standards you would have maybe labelled us as hoodies, or some sort of description bearing that stereotypical look. This would bring out a different side to me, a mischievous or troubled side, we would do all the things that you shouldn't. One summer evening we somehow had managed to lay our hands on some paint from our school's art department storage room. It was about 10.30pm, sun was setting as it does, people had been out having BBQs, fun in their gardens etc. Along the back of this row of houses there was a path that would connect with other paths as well as the main road like a maze of routes. There were four of us armed with these paint tubes of about a 1 litre-sized bottle. We noticed that somebody had left their washing out on the washing line, well, we just couldn't resist, so there we were squirting these tubes of paint all over this washing; trousers, shirts, underwear, dresses. Not stopping there, we then proceeded on to their greenhouse... Laugh! I don't think I stopped laughing for weeks after that, all I could imagine in my head was the person opening their back door and not really believing their eyes at what they thought they were seeing. Just to clear things up, it was child friendly paint so it was washable, I only hope they realised that before possibly throwing the items into the bin.

Thinking back now on a lot of things that I did when I was younger, it was because I was looking for recognition to be accepted, to fit in and to be seen as normal rather than the different kid, because that's how it was a lot of the time. Obviously, my primary years I never noticed things, just got on with it. As I moved into my teenage years it was evident that other kids' views of me were different and was made apparent on a number of occasions. I see it now with kids, they make comments to each other without really thinking, those comments can be quite hurtful to the recipient which can run deep if the other person is of a softer caring nature. That's just how I was, I struggled to understand why other kids were inclined towards me this way, I mean I hadn't caused them any harm, nor said anything bad towards them, yet I would still receive the nasty comments, or overhear the odd word that would be clearly about myself. This would start to build trepidation, I would begin to form a complexity about myself which in turn would then affect the way that I was around people, only ever so slightly that you probably wouldn't see, but over time it would in fact become a huge issue.

I would start to think that people were talking about me, in school and out of school. It was the days before social media so I can only imagine how things can be now for anyone that is going through anything like this. I would start to question myself, my worth, did people just put up with me, did they just really want me not to show up when we used to meet as a group. There were times when I went to where we would usually meet up to find that they weren't there, and when later I caught up with them they would just come out with some excuse as to why they were not there. As times goes on you learn to live with it, yeah there were times when it was horrible. I struggled to comprehend why it was like this, bulling in school wasn't really in the public eye back then as it is now, you would get called names, occasionally chased, but you would just take it, just get on with things. It's only now when I look at it that I can identify that it was bulling.

My conclusion to friends now is that some people will be a part of your life, they will either stay or they will go, it's the experiences that you have during that time that count.

Chapter 16
Savage

There becomes a point in time when you feel that you have found your meaning, your purpose in life, I've never really had a plan B. Well, for the last 37 years since my accident I feel I've been living in my plan B. It was only really the past 12 months or so that I started to gather a sense of the direction that I felt comfortable to invest in, the one quality that I was more than happy to boast about. I am a good person doing what I want, in helping others! Have I found myself, may be my plan B is actually my plan A! Unfortunately, it was to come crashing down on me the morning of October 9th, 2018.

It was just a normal Tuesday morning, after a quick session on the indoor training bike, I threw my clothes on, and made the short journey to my place of work. I had recently moved house as I wanted to be closer to the school that I was working at to cut my travel time down, it made sense in the long run. I turned up and went on with my duties as a teaching assistant, with my first two lessons assisting two year eight students with their French and geography. After those first two lessons it was break time in which I went to our usual place that all the teaching assistant staff would meet for a coffee each morning. I was greeted by one of the secretaries that informed me that the deputy head needed to speak to me, and would I wait behind after break, my anxieties instantly kicked in as they usually do if anything in my life becomes slightly out of routine. As I waited questions were spinning in my head as to what she possibly wanted to talk to me about at this time of the day. I was left waiting for around 20 minutes before I was called into the boardroom, instantly I knew there was something wrong. As I sat down the sinking feeling hit me, I was never any good at dealing with situations like this, always thinking that I have done something wrong whenever I am placed in front of anyone senior to myself, my thought processes are slow, I struggle to keep up with things that are spoken to me in stressful situations, but this was to be horrific. It was put to me that a concern had been brought to their attention due to my conduct involving my previous employer. Baffled slightly by this I tried to make sense of what was being said to me, it had been brought up that I had broken rules of conduct over a message of support that I had sent to a former student that I had worked with after they had messaged me regarding some concerns that they were having. I was confused as this was nothing to do with my current employer, nor of the type of work that they were employing me for in my new position. After around 20 minutes of explaining the situation it was then put to me that I would be suspended pending an inquiry. it was at this point that I sank into the floor, things that were said after that point I wasn't hearing, the trepidation hit me, feeling perplexed I didn't know what to say or do. The two staff members that were in the room, the deputy head and the human resources person seemed very confused themselves, they knew very little of the work that I had done at my previous school, the effort that had gone into it over the whole eight months that I was there. Feeling alone in that chair as they spoke to me, I was then escorted off the school premises via the side door like a convicted criminal walking into a prison cell. I sat in my car trying to piece together what had just happened, insurmountable! That's all that I could think, *How can I deal with this, where do I turn,* I had no one. A week went by before I was called back for another meeting; a week in which I hardly slept; I didn't really eat much. In the back of my mind I could see that there was no harm caused in my actions to return the message that I had received, but on the second meeting I felt a feeling of complete consternation, it was explained to me that after a midweek meeting with my previous employer that further information had been received. This just threw me into a whirlwind of turmoil as it was evident that lies were being thrown into the proceedings, it was turning into a witch hunt, this heightened my anxieties to a level never experienced before. I had been assured that the enquiry would be carried out in the best possible way, that I would be given a fair opportunity to put my side of things across. The human resources person at the school that had been assigned as my designated person that was there for myself as support, should I have needed to call her at any point would be my soul contact. I felt unsafe, scared, my belief and confidence that I would be supported through the process by two people that were already making mistakes suddenly turned to fear, in fact after that second meeting I was not so sure about my confidences in any of the organisations and agencies involved. Firstly the previous High school that I worked at that first brought up the concern which started this process were now throwing even more ill-founded accusations into the mix, which when I asked for more information surrounding the matter my correspondences were ignored. They also retracted a reference that they had supplied to my new employer, giving no real reason as to why, which baffled me as the work that I had completed there was nothing but successful. My only conclusion being that as I was a personal friend of the senior deputy head teacher and his family, then having a personal relationship meant that for him to supply the reference, was in the first place probably breaking one of his own school policies, therefore leaving him in somewhat of an embarrassing situation. So in order to save himself from any disciplinary action, it was obviously far easier for them to void the reference which would in turn clean their own doorstep. What really hurt from this was how he ceased his contact with myself as of that point. He judged me, after almost three years of friendship, he just treated me like an outcast, like it meant nothing, I just hope as a person of faith that he so claimed to be, that he is able to live with himself and explain to his family his actions. I suppose I already knew what sort of person he was after going to him early in the year with a note that a couple of students had handed to me regarding my work with them, which stated that they were grateful for my work with them, that they felt that I was someone that they could talk to if they needed a sounding board during the school day, and that they had been inspired to do better at their work. He read this note after I took it to him to which he replied that he could make it disappear. I was that shocked to say the least by his reaction that I was unable to speak, I mean here we had evidence that some students were progressing in their own well-being, yet he was sat there with more interest at putting it into the bin and disregarding his students' progress.

With things in that second meeting just starting to stack up against me, the second accusation that was issued was just a complete lie, with no factual evidence being presented. At that point my anxieties were starting to make themselves known, even the human resources support network of my employer seemed to be taking a backseat at this point which left me feeling isolated. The meeting was more of a scene from the TV show chuckle vision with the way the deputy head and the human resources were bouncing the questions at myself. The whole set up from start to finish was very poor in showing any sort of support or engagement towards myself. My stresses were starting to take a hold of me, the affects that came with that started to take their toll, waking in the night feeling very frustrated that information was starting to become misconstrued in this process, that nobody was actually interested in my side of the events. I was acting on my own behalf as I did not trust anyone to act in the right way, I made countless phone calls, sent email correspondents to try and get to the bottom of what was actually going on. Eventually I managed to organise a meeting with the local authority designated officer for the independent safeguarding services that had informed the high school in the first place, instructing them to suspend me whilst the inquiry was going on. My first encounter with her was that of absolute buffoonery, she had limited information about the case which I found very poor considering her position of authority, any factual information that I presented to her caught her unawares which she was unable to comment on, it started to become clear at that point I was going to have a tough time as a lot of the initial information had been misinterpreted.

I recall going home after that meeting with her thinking how on earth are these people that are involved in this inquiry actually working the positions that they are within their organisations, they just didn't seem capable. I was starting to feel that not only was I being failed, but also the youngsters which they are supposed to be looking out for.

When I started to ask questions, no one had any definitive answers, even after going away to have more meetings with the previous high school they could still not provide the answers. The shocking moment during that process was when the local authority designated officer had to ask her work colleague the address of where she worked when I phoned to request the address to send an important letter to, I was absolutely dumbfounded at just so much incompetence there was from all parties.

After weeks of feeling unsupported I was called in for the final meeting with the head teacher of the dean trust for the outcome of their enquiry. I figured it was only a matter of time, and after just 20 minutes my fate was decided. My contract was terminated with immediate effect due to misconduct. I was devastated, how had this ended in such a mess! Again, I was escorted out of the school in the same manner as of the first meeting, sick and vial are the only words I can use to describe it. I knew things had been handled wrong, but it felt out of my hands. That afternoon I had arranged a meeting once again with the 'LADO' (Local Authority Designated Officer). I was already feeling low and dejected as I didn't really know what to expect from the next meeting. It was all a bit of a blur, my self-esteem at a non-existent state. I sat and listened to her jabbering on about how I should think about taking something else up as a career, that maybe inspiring young people wasn't for me, and then going on to say that I wasn't professional in my duties.

I am actually motivated by my duties, I stop at nothing to get things done, world champion, world record holder, Paralympic medallist, you don't get to that level by going home and switching off, you stay and commit more time, you leave no stone unturned, you strive to be the best in the world, and you will do whatever it takes. That's the mind of a champion, that's the mentality that I carry into anything that I do regardless of boundaries. Working absolute frontline as a support worker you have to ask yourself some big questions sometimes. I'd look in the mirror each morning, I'd ask myself, *Am I willing to take the hit, am I willing to sacrifice everything for somebody else to live, to make sure somebody else's life is that bit better?* The answer is the same every day, that's why I'm the best at what I do. So the professionalism of those officer workers, box tickers and pen pushers are not even on the scale. In the line of work that I do my ethics mean a lot to me, I will stand by them time and time again.

The negativity that I was starting to feel in that meeting was overwhelming, you start to realise that the authorities aren't interested, the walls were starting to crumble in on me, it all became very confusing. It was like I was talking, but no one was listening. I spoke in depth of the work that I had done, the fact that I had stopped a young person from taking their own life, but the chair of the meeting wasn't interested. Her actual comment was "There are still plenty of children succeeding in schools," like that child's life didn't even warrant a minute's thought, like they were second rate. So disheartening to have witnessed all these goings on. That last comment from someone in a position of authority just broke me, all I could think about was the hard work all of the students that I have worked with have put in to the work, some of the most difficult times that some of them have faced, and sat opposite me someone now just disregarding them and their lives.

I left that meeting at my lowest, things became worse as the weeks went by. The period of time that followed that meeting, the conglomeration of the weeks leading up to it would have tested even the most resilient of people. For myself it was a time that I never want to go through ever again, dragging me to the depths of wanting to take my own life. I was at the end, I really just had run out of options to put things right, I lost my direction, I didn't care about a thing, nothing made sense. I went missing for five days, I was sleeping in my car, just wandering aimlessly in the day time from one town to another not really giving a shit about life, being in fear of fear, I did literally have no thought process going on. Eventually I was found by the police that had obviously been searching for me.

Saving someone's life gave me a tremendous sense of purpose. The time, the effort that I invested with that one person to keep them alive and smiling is just something that I will never forget, but then to have it thrown at you, then used against you in the way that it was, just completely fucked me to a point in which I broke into pieces as I just couldn't take anymore.

In the aftermath of what I had endured as a result of the local authority and the two schools involved in the whole situation which ultimately resulted in me losing my new job position was horrendous. It didn't stop there though, it had affected my private life to which I was left with no contact with three people that I had so much time for that I had been spending each weekend with. I was left with nothing but my own thoughts of misery. Someone had decided to just take everything from my life without a second thought!

Try to imagine everything that you believe in, all that you respect, something you have built up over six years that you have so much passion for just being rubbished by others. Add in 30 months of your own personal life having been shattered in front of your eyes, to then have that taken from you just like that by an organisation and people that don't know you, it just finishes you completely beyond comprehension. I can't describe the emptiness that I was feeling, the frustration of not knowing where I could go or what I could do.

I've always worked hard to achieve, always placed other people first, yet I always seem to be the one to get the rough end of the stick. I may be selfish in my sport, have that determined mind, but on the other hand I will do anything for anyone, try to remember my manners, try to be generally nice, and treat others like I would like to be treated myself, but this showed that it doesn't pay to be nice, there's no advantage to being a good person anymore, no one cares, it's just not appreciated!

Day after day I just didn't want to go on, my anxieties telling me there seems to be no light at the end of the tunnel, I had limited interactions with other people as I just didn't want to talk, I was trying to juggle everything that was happening. I would question every aspect which was just going around in my head 24 hours a day like a fair ground ride, I'd get in bed at night to find that I was unable to rid my mind of the despair. A visit to my doctor only resulted in him prescribing me anti-depressants that brought even more uncertainty, feeling embarrassed at the thought of people knowing that I was taking medication for mental issues. I was still trying everything that I could to stay positive, to change the situation that I found myself in, yet I just seemed to be getting more shit thrown at me which was getting to the point where I started to self-harm as it was my only release from the anguish.

For almost five months I was feeling like this with no progress. The little sleep that I would succumb to at night was sparse, just the sounds of a fleeting clock ticking the seconds by, then the hours until daylight reappears through the crack in the curtain presenting another repetition of the days and weeks that had gone by. I felt a prisoner in my own mind, locked away with the inner screams that nobody else could hear, how much more would or could I have taken. That determined little person that I was in that hospital bed after my accident was really up against the demons of depression. it was a living hell, waking each morning not wanting the day to exist, laying there with my eyes fixed on the ceiling with not so much as a thought for breathing, that blank feeling that I'd never experienced before in my life, then it hits you all over again as to why I am feeling like this. Then realising that there is nothing that I can do, thoughts just running their own party inside my head to the point that I wanted to scream, I'd venture out of bed having slept in my clothes from the previous day because like today, yesterday was just a repartition of the last. I'd move from the bed to the chair, managing to somehow make a coffee en route after trying to find a clean cup from the mounting array of dishes from around the kitchen sink from days gone by. The days almost turned to an automatic process, with no agenda. How I got through each day I don't know. What was keeping me going? There must have been something in my subconscious mind that was keeping me holding onto life. My conscious mind was just slowly destroying itself to the point that no process was even possible, even to think of starting some sort of thinking process wasn't there, just emptiness. As I'd sit there in the chair, numb, my only feeling was hurt like I'd never felt before. A faint thought would pop into my mind about the phone numbers that my doctor had passed to me to call if I desperately needed to talk to someone that would maybe sway me from doing myself any harm or worse. I would then find myself once again suddenly go blank with the dull sounds of the television in the background that were just there to kill the total silence of what I was going through.

Over the years I have read or heard about different people that have been going through difficult times in their lives, pretty desperate places, and for those that have even attempted to end it all, must have only had nowhere to turn. I can now see from what I was going through, how you can be pushed to a place where there is nothing. I didn't really have a full understanding of depression, how it manifests and clouds you. It is in fact a complete feeling of its own. For myself I can see that I have struggled on and off with it for years, I'm still struggling to find the words to explain it. One word I keep referring back to is worthlessness! From the minute I opened my eyes in the morning until I eventually drifted off to sleep at whatever time that may have been at night. I use the word sleep, simply it is more like my eyes would be closed with all the thoughts still going on behind my eyelids. I turned and rolled all night, shifting my head on the pillow to try to find some sort of salvation, hoping that I would find that point in the pillow where my thoughts would soak away leaving me in comfort for at least a couple of hours. With no such luck I just had to juggle with my innermost feelings, the deepest darkest and some of the most harrowing perceptions of what was actually going on in my life at that moment.

I just seemed to be in a deep depression of two battles; one of my conscious being and the other with my subconscious thoughts running a wild with an unpredictable charge whenever I try to switch off from for even just a second, leaving me in a seesaw momentum 24 hours a day. I'd stare at the phone numbers of crisis teams, contemplating to dial the numbers, but with a hesitation of the thought of speaking to a stranger, not knowing who will pick up at the other end, will it be a male, a female, what questions would they ask. I started to fill my mind of different excuses not to make the call like I had been doing for weeks, even talking to the doctor didn't feel right as I'd never hear the answers that I wanted to hear, never those comforting words that I long to hear somebody speak, that hug or reaching out of a hand. Even after talking to the police the night I was found, then being issued a safeguarding support officer that called around from time to time. I still didn't feel the answers were out there, then the thoughts reached the end point, the worthlessness of being somewhere that the only way that this will go away was to just wish that I wouldn't wake up in the mornings.

So I have to try to rebuild my entire life yet again, not only was my future career. Working with youngsters placed on hold, also my personal life with three people that I was spending time with as of the connections that surrounded this utter mess, absolute ludicrous is all I can say. I still struggle with a lot of things, trying to make sense of it all, searching, trying to put things right, but it's all in slow steps, every one of those steps can be extremely frustrating. Nine times out of 10 they don't provide me with the answer that I am seeking, a local safeguarding officer was appointed to keep a watch as I was deemed at risk to myself and others which left my emotional tent crowded with people that I didn't really want around me. We have to keep going on though, keep moving forward, albeit a lot of the time I just wanted it to end. I'd ask myself, 'What would that achieve?' It's a really difficult question. Mentally, you feel completely done with nothing more to offer, and that would be right, for anyone that has, or is going through mental health issues, they are the ones that only truly know, can comprehend the emptiness, the end of the timeline feeling.

Only yesterday I was sat in a café trying to write some pages of this book when things just became purposeless, nothing had any meaning. I looked around at other people; nothing was registering, just sat where I was, I couldn't even think of my next move. I looked over to the balcony, the thoughts ran through my mind of just stepping over, no one would know, it would be over in a flash, no feeling anymore, no knot in my stomach getting tighter each day because of the torturous feelings that were going around in my mind, the sickening feeling that I experienced each day was unbearable. What was keeping me from ending my life, was I waiting for a final outcome, was there a glimmer of hope that was keeping me from taking such a catastrophic form of action, or was it just a case of waiting for another day of more low feelings to finally tilt me to completely losing all of my inner senses, those senses that for the past 41 years have built the strong-minded person that I have been through the times when I needed them to say that I will get there in the end. Never before had I been in such a desperate situation that I'd be classed as a missing person, been searched for, never before had I wanted to end it all. Thinking back about the situation with the female student and how she now must have been feeling with her own turmoil, yet she was able to bring herself back. I look at all the days when I spoke with her, the days when I chased around trying to fix situations for her, to make her days just that little more bearable to cope with. How did she manage to turn things around? Then it hit me; it's because I gave her time, I had the ability to help her, so why was I unable to help myself. Surely if I could do it for others then I must be able to do it for myself, the quality was already in me, it's nothing new, I just had to dig that bit deeper to find it within my suppressed soul buried away under all of the anguish and clutter that had been the catalyst for all this chaos. I remembered a quote from her, "We may encounter many defeats, but we must not be defeated." Obviously, it's a quote by Maya Angelou, but She was using this, just maybe it was something that she believed in to use in her life, to assist her in her troubles.

The darkest places of our lives, how do we make the deal with ourselves, I had to somehow drag myself back. Life is too short. I had to find something to focus on even if it was a temporary measure to allow some thinking space. With my anxieties so prominent each day they would leave me in a state where I was just on the floor, unable to move. I found that over the months while this was going on that I was also eating a lot of quick and easy junk food, downing chocolate bars or anything that was high in sugar as it would give me that lift, albeit short lived. I would be eating takeaways three and four times a week to make me feel better, it would be a short hit of a comfort blanket effect, then this would trigger the guilt. My anxieties would awaken, I was making a terrible situation even more catastrophic. This would then plummet me into a deeper depression. I was ashamed when I looked in the mirror, what was looking back at me was not the same person that I used to be, both physically and mentally, downhearted and completely broken, this was not like me at all. Only I could fix this. I was left with two choices, go into some sort of rehab, or to lock myself down, deal with it by myself and turn myself to doing something that I knew I could do to my best. My nutrition was the starting point, I needed to kick all the shite that I was consuming, after all, if you are getting the right nutrients into your body, then your system will start to pick itself up. Sounds easy. I can tell you, it's not in any way, shape or form easy. Kicking the sugar, the high fats were a struggle, my body would be shaking like a dog-shitting razor blade.

After a few weeks of stabilising my diet I started to feel somewhat able to approach my day with a little more of an upbeat mood. I still was having the darkened moments, but I knew I had to stick at it no matter how bad it became. My next step was to incorporate some exercise. My Wattbike and altitude simulator had been sat dormant for longer than I could remember. With these tools I could accelerate things without the daunting feeling of going out into public through fear of panic attacks and anxious feelings showing themselves in a fit of rage and destruction. They were waiting, looking for their way in, a quick easy route to run wild and push me down. I was one step ahead of them each day. After a few weeks of exercise mixed with the correct food intake, my confidence was starting to build, I had not looked at my body in the mirror for around three weeks as I was scared of seeing not a lot of difference. I plucked up the courage to analyse the outline of my reflection. I could see that physically I was starting to change, for the first time in months I could feel that change. My road bike was sat begging to see the tarmac again. Seizing this moment, I swiftly riffled through the cupboard in search of my winter biking clothing, climbed into it and stepped out for the first time. As I whizzed through the first few streets of where I live, I was feeling excitement as I turned the peddles, my adrenaline was fuelling my leg speed, as I dropped down one of the hills into the village of Shevington. I rapidly picked up speed, the crisp cold biting winter air rushing past my ears, my eyes watering trying to adjust to this reborn activity in the fresh air. I could have ridden all day. Unfortunately, after around 30 minutes my legs would give way to exhaustion of being unconditioned to the level at which I was asking of them.

The following day from the minute I opened my eyes all I wanted to do was get out on the road and ride. What was this get up and go attitude feeling that I was having! It was making me feel jovial even though my fitness levels were pretty second hand. It was making that difference to my mindset, that progress that I had been in search of. My altitude simulator was to be my next hit. I knew from my past training programmes that it makes an exceptional difference to the way you feel. Structure was starting to form in the things that I was consciously doing. Subconsciously I was still pretty unbalanced, not so much as I had been, but nevertheless I couldn't ignore the times when I would be sat in the chair on an evening with nothing to do when the little anxieties would try and creep back in, trying to nudge me off my path. It was really testing as they would present themselves as true fact, then rapidly turn on me. How was I to totally eradicate them. I had put these things in place now to fill bits of my day in a way that would fill me with a feeling of achievement, but they still seem to be able to overhaul me in a way, stamp on any good feeling that I was having. I have boxes of anti-depressants that I didn't want to succumb to, I already take enough medication to knock an elephant sideways, so this for me was a last resort! But was it the only thing that was going to totally kill off my anxieties and allow me to go all day without feeling the need to push my own head into a pillow?

I am not one to back down, and once had the determination to battle through most things. This I could see was one of them moments, it just required a little more determination to break through to the other side. I had made these first few steps which have proved to be a valued medication and I'm sure that with more steps like this that I can reach a point where I can re-introduced myself as a better person.

Towards the end I received correspondence from the DBS (Data Barring Service) that I had been in touch with throughout this traumatic process. They were the one organisation that dealt with the circumstances with a professional attitude, stating that no wrong doing on my behalf had taken place, and that I was clear to carry on working in the professional field of supporting youngsters and vulnerable people. This was by far the best news that I had received throughout this whole farce of an enquiry. It now left me in a somewhat slightly subdued feeling that yes, I want to go back into helping youngsters with the challenges they may be facing, or the mental health impact that schooling may be having on them, but at the same time with the way the school policies and structures are in this current climate then I feel that I would not be able to achieve the same level of success that I had been doing for fear that my work may be looked upon as stepping over the boundaries. Regulations and policies need to undergo a dramatic overhaul, more so for frontline support staff in order that a break through on the current mental health crisis that has invaded our schools to the degree that it has done can be tackled successfully.

Chapter 17
Empires over Education

An awful lot of schools now are becoming self-governing academies such as sponsored academies, or Academy Trusts which mean they do not have to follow the National curriculum but do have to include the core subjects of Mathematics and English. This leaves them to operate freely outside of local authority control which allows them the freedom over their finances, teachers' pay and conditions etc., They can, however, tap into funding from the government that would have previously been held back by the local authority to provide extra services across the school, such as help for children with special educational needs. On paper this looks extremely good, big pots of funds to spend how and wherever they like. With my involvement as a member of a school board of governors I have had a small insight to how curtain structures are run from the top, the board of governors and trustees where the classroom setting hardly is of any discussion as the main focus is figures and grades within the local and national area. Schools now are run by business people trying to build an empire for themselves, chasing their own single-minded ambitions, whether that be local business person of the month, the year or some kind of recognition for their services to education, and more recently I heard of the chasing of an honour and even a knighthood by some. This is a totally separate issue to mental health issues in school, but as a collective the impact is felt at grassroots, constant pushing from teachers' impacts on the students that are quite often undeveloped to deal with such mental pressure and rightly so.

For any young person school can be seen as a place for learning, maturing, making friends and growing up, but unfortunately the reality for a lot of youngsters can be quite different. School can be the most challenging place of our lives. Years 10 and 11 can feel almost impossible, a conveyor belt of test after test and exam after exam with mounting pressure on the approach to each crucial period because of the expectation thrust upon them from the teachers who themselves have been placed under mountains of pressure by senior leaders that quite often set unrealistic targets based on the previous year's results. From comparing the class of say 2018 to the class of 2019 without taking into account the vast social background differences between a lot of the students. From my work in schools and witnessing not just the effect such structure has on the students, but also the unimaginable pressure that the teaching staff are placed under to try and achieve these results to ultimately make the school look good on paper is heart-breaking. Children are suffering right across the spectrum because of how schools are being run now. In the working 9 to 5 world, a chairperson will discuss the running of their company with senior management teams and they then will hand out predictions and forecasts then to line managers. These line mangers will speak with the front-line staff who they then expect to carry out the work that will ultimately gain those greater results and figures first issued by the chair or business owner. My point in the above is that the frontline staff are of adult age and mentally developed enough to be able to comprehend the pressures that they may or may not be feeling in being asked to produce a better standard of work and results. At the age of 14, 15 and 16 the mind of a student can be very different with some being more mature than others as we all know, but still the pressures and expectation in gaining greater results are mounting each year on the undeveloped minds of children. Every child learns in their own unique way and if by the middle of year nine your prediction of GCSE scores that are worked out by senior leadership staff show that your grades come the time of sitting the GCSE exam is that of a value below a five then you are unfortunately placed in a situation that the school rather than invest a little more time into you to help you achieve a higher grade actually devalues your worthwhile the predicted six to nine achievers are actually invested in more. Surely from purely just a business point of view that most of these trustees and governors are now, that are running our schools, wouldn't it be more viable to invest heavily in the lower predicted achievers to bring them up to speed which in turn would increase scores as a whole rather than put more investment into the higher achievers that are already quite capable of hitting those predictions on their own ability and self-esteem.

From my point of the work that I have been a part of and working with these so-called predicted low achieving students, which I think is disgraceful to label them in this way, they are all capable of achieving high scores in the main subjects, the none or very low investment of these students from mid-year nine onwards can only enlighten the challenges that some of them may already have going on in their lives. Mental health is as import as exams, from year seven schools should take more responsibility for students in lower sets, instead of placing them all under one umbrella right through to year 11, kids already feel under pressure socially from a young age so why not show them something different that they will embrace and realise that school instead of being an environment that they feel pressured in, that it's actually somewhere where they feel less pressured, somewhere they can feel they want to be because the right people are there for them and not the results that they can produce.

The turnaround of students that I worked with was phenomenal. A lot many were in year nine, so that middle year, somewhere maturing faster than others, some academically had so much to offer, but because of the current system of predicting their GCSE results come two years times they would have most probably have missed out on that investment that would have possibly seen them jump into that six to nine bracket. With this comes the added pressure which can lead to mental health problems like has been in the press now for so long with nobody really doing an awful lot to address it. There are all the campaigns and organisations that are around to support but are well and truly overrun. Things need to be addressed by the government to not only ease this situation, but to stop the likes of high flying business people using the system to chase their own ambitions of being the heads of empires and turning schools into corporate cash registers. This leaves so many children swimming in pools of treacle once they reach a certain age by the schools devaluing them should they not be capable of hitting that unknown score, worked out from a table that can be somewhat corrupt as I also have learnt from over hearing conversations by senior leaders by the fact that some schools, when it comes to releasing data for national league tables, only actually publish their top results to gain themselves a higher position on the results table. The majority of those results have been gathered by the top set students that have been heavily invested in from year 10, in other words by not releasing their full data they look super polished, portraying a better image for investors and trustees, so even more investment for the top set students, pushing the lower set children into the background, with the main chairperson looking ever so better, creeping closer to their honour and recognition for services to education.

Students are not the only ones to feel the pressures which are leading to mental health issues as a result of the ambitions of others, teachers and staff are also becoming victim to the torturous results and numbers game seeking that are thrust upon them from higher departments. This then filters down into the classroom. I have felt it as I have sat there working with students, teachers loosing track of the lesson, or rushing through certain tasks as they are running behind, desks overrun with mounting work and stacked high of books ready for marking, lesson plans on posted notes stuck to the PC monitor for reference. Unable to take a full lunch or forgoing the midmorning break due to playing catch up as of the mounds of work needed to get through. This then leads to concentration levels being exhausted come the lessons with the lower set students. The unpredictability of some of the students, their mood swings and so-called behavioural issues due to them themselves feeling the pressure placed upon them makes them act in a way that is deemed as disruptive by the school, often resulting in the teacher having that student removed and subsequently punished by the school for being naughty. The child then instead of being supported ends up sitting in isolation, a room staring at a wall or a screen, feeling alone, anxious and singled out, they then become unable to comprehend what he or she has done wrong, and rightly so. The actions of the teacher having stemmed from their own feeling of pressures placed on them which trustees and the like fail to see. The frontline work that is now involved is desperately needed for already vulnerable children to successfully achieve without going through the mental health problems, complexities and endeavours it brings that they have little understanding of which can lead to self-harm issues, a catalogue of complications and can sometimes end with a loss of a young life.

My first-hand experience at saving a young person's life in circumstances not too dissimilar from this, having a positive effect on two others within the same school was only the tip of the iceberg. This came at great cost to myself; it has had adverse effects post the work that I had achieved. The frustrations at all the lack of understanding from the authorities and schools, the utter disregard and shamefully shallow respect shown to the lives of the children that worked so hard to better themselves. Not for one minute would I change any of the work that I did, nor would I think twice about doing it again, my drive is to help young people achieve, live the life that they all should be able to enjoy and go on to prosper from without the added pressure cast upon them by adults chancing figures and results in order to fulfil their own riches in a place where kids should feel that they want to come to learn about everything that they need once they reach exam age, and not feel the pressure of something they haven't yet experienced.

This impacted on myself more than I thought at the time, it was only once I started to understand my own reasons for my mental health issues, where they were stemming from, that I was able to see the bigger picture of what is happening. I'm an adult yet I let these things fester inside of me, even when I knew that I hadn't done anything wrong, it still didn't stop my mind fuelling the frustrations of not being understood through the different organisations not being clear with each other which runs true on a lot of things. It must be three or even four times more difficult for young people of today in school.

A young boy I happened to work with by chance last year had some big challenges going on in his life, only to be made worse by the school in their actions in the way that they handled a situation that will have only added to his mental health issues. It was just a standard afternoon, or so I thought, there had been an incident in the school library. The senior staff had closed off the corridors to stop any other child from entering the vicinity, as I peered through the widow in the door I could see a young boy being man handled by four male members of staff out of the library and down the corridor. The boy was obviously in some distress at being held as he was unable to resist. The very next day I was asked if I would speak with this boy who was 13 and possibly do some work around helping him with his frustrations. It was only after I had spent a good hour with him that afternoon that I would learn that this boy had a lot of very intricate anxieties that stemmed from past history. At the age of 10 he witnessed from his bedroom window his father beat up another person which affected him quite severely that had left him feeling angry, frustrated and feeling pressure in other parts of his life. On discovering this my thoughts returned to the previous day, and the way that the situation was handled in moving him from the school library. Surely the school must have been aware of this boy's history, and that being the case why would you then warrant it suitable for four male teachers to physically remove him. It could have only added more feeling of turmoil to his fragile mental state for sure. This is where school policies need to be looked at. From my understanding every school is slightly different with regards to protocol in the way that they deal with such situations, but from a mental health point of view the above was very disturbing to witness, to then work with the boy, listen to his story and then reflect on the way that his circumstances were handled in this harrowing ordeal.

Mental health and well-being, it's something that they don't teach you in school, there are so many basic processes in life that school doesn't give you that you really need just to give you the essentials of basic understanding. It's an area that I now am very passionate about that would give kids of today a better understanding of life rather than just the standard processes that schools offer currently. I mean I'm not going to completely overhaul the curriculum, but I really wonder why schools don't have these things in place, I mean as soon as you leave school you're sort of just thrown quite literally in the deep end. They never teach about how to cope with even the smallest of stresses or problem solving, but put you under huge pressure to achieve when they haven't even covered the basics about the how and why we feel under pressure and how to deal with it.

The whole safeguarding policies that are currently in place in schools, what are they there for? Are they really there to protect children and vulnerable adults, or are they in place to protect the adults from the children? So many children are feeling alone and isolated because they feel that they cannot approach any adults for help which I have been privy to witness. That then leaves them in a somewhat dark place of mental health and wellbeing, a feeling of insurmountable consternation. I have witnessed this on so many occasions over the past twelve months leaving me feeling that I was unable to step back and let things continue. I would be spoken to by senior leaders who would say not to become too involved, always watch out not to leave yourself in a classroom with a child as you could end up being accused of something, it would be put across in a way that fear would set in that you almost couldn't talk to the students. It was bad, they had labelled the kids, safeguarding themselves as adults and isolating the students. I recall after I had been spoken to in this way walking into a classroom for a session with a student and feeling awful, the words of a senior deputy head made me feel that I didn't want to be there anymore, he had thrust upon me this image that all kids were bad. After a while of fighting with my thoughts and his ideas of how he perceived the students in his school, I realised that what I stood for meant more, my beliefs in helping people without pre judging them were stronger. So, who are we safeguarding? You tell me?

Chapter 18
A Saving Grace

So I guess this is where I tell you what I have learned. My conclusion, well, my conclusion is that worry and anxiety is baggage, life is too short to worry about a thing. I say this but I'm sure there will be more testing times throughout the rest of my life, when I just think back to when I was younger I used to think memories were meant to be solely about happy times, when in fact they can be just about literally anything that your mind absorbs and stores away until such time you feel the need to reflect, to take a step back and analyse certain aspects of not just your own life, but other people's lives that you have had the privilege to be part of which is what has brought me to where I am today, right now sat in front of this screen typing out everything that has gone before this moment in time. The student that I worked with to save her life is the whole reason as to why I literally decided to sit down and write these 18 chapters about my life, the story has always been there. I've just made every excuse for fear of failing in my writing, I just needed a kick of inspiration and she showed that despite all of the turmoil that she was facing and the hurdles that kept being placed in front of her that inwardly she too had the same single-minded determination that I had from when I was just five years old. That one single attribute changed her life, it saved her from possibly a totally different outcome. For me it was like seeing a mirror image of myself lay in that hospital bed in September 82, feeling those inner screams, nobody hearing them and taking notice that I wanted to achieve. For her I'm just glad I was there at a time in her life when she really needed someone to listen, just the few words or the belief that I offered not only built her a solid foundation for her future, but it also gave me a new inspiration to write. At the time it sort of passed unnoticed to me as my work was to make sure she stayed alive as it was with others that I worked with, to create her own path to be able to successfully achieve. That was my number one priority, it was just in this intense period of anxieties that I have been put through for what has now been close to six months that all the parts of this mammoth jigsaw came together and gave me that clear vision of what you have just read. I'd always wanted to write an autobiography, but always came up with the same excuse; doubting my ability to just sit, write and think of aspect of my life that I have been through, well write the parts that related to what I have tried to bring across.

I'm really excited in a way, maybe in 10 or 20 years I will pick up a book that will be written by her, documenting her life, all the achievements and experiences that she has had the fortune to make and reap the rewards from.

I look down at my own left arm, the scars from my own self harming which will be a reminder not just of my own troubles and challenges, but also the day that she was standing there in front of me as she rolled up her sleeve to reveal her arm weeping with blood from the cuts and scrapes, the results of a dark and isolated space that she could see no way out of. There is always opportunity, always an answer if you search hard enough and use the power from within. The brain is the best computer that you will ever own, it has no limits, we just need to believe in ourselves and believe in others because we are human. We are the species that have the ability to do anything that we want to, but most of us chose to sit at home, we chose to make the excuse that we are too tired, that we don't have the time or we let television dictate our daily time schedule or have that extra time in bed as it's easy just to lay there and do nothing. We even use that excuse as a status when summer time officially ends by announcing on television that we get an extra hour in bed when we have to alter the clocks back when really it should be put across as we get an extra hour added on to our lives for free. Think of that concept, how amazing! I have never really understood the whole concept of the clocks changing, I heard it to assist the farmers with light, well, I'll let you in on a secret, it's bull, farm machinery today are fitted with more lights than Blackpool!

Imagine being close to death and someone saying to you, I'm giving you an extra hour to live. What would you do with that one hour; would you lay down, snuggle into the pillow leaving your mind to wander, filling your final hour with undesirable thoughts, driving you to despair, or would you embrace it, filling it with as much as you could. I think I know what most of you would say, so why have that extra hour in bed? Take that hour, that 60 minutes, that 3600 seconds and go do something, you can achieve so much in that time that will give you satisfaction and a sense of accomplishment. We are given two legs, two arms, two eyes, ears and two nostrils, but we give too many excuses not to do anything.

If I calculate the time, I have spent helping young people over the last twelve months it would run into 100s of hours, if not thousands, with a lot of that time being for free. I didn't do what I did for a paycheque, nor a comment on my CV. I did it because of my ethics, I have a passion for helping people, I have this natural ability to be able to connect with today's youth, for all the teaching staff, all the support staff in many of the schools that I have worked in, the teachers could not connect with the students due to the pressures that they were feeling in their own place of work, their time being limited, that's why I was brought in, because I was the best at what I did, I was sourced because of my ability to change lives.

For me I realise that the anxieties that I have of my own will never go away, they will always be a part of my life, in a sense a companion that I learn to live with, they have taken me to the darkest place in my life over the past five or so months. I allowed them to get a hold of me too much that led me to a depressive state, to the point of suicidal thoughts, it took me a long time to work things out, to figure why I was letting my own thoughts destroy me like a self-destruct mechanism, when really I should have been able to control them in a much better way being of adult age. We often blame ourselves; we question our own ability far too much; we underestimate just how powerful we actually are. I still struggle with things, I would be lying if I told you that I was totally cured, but I can deal with things differently now, my state of being is somewhat altered through not only what I have learnt about myself, but also other people. My trust in people was pretty low before all this happened. It's a terrible feeling to have. It's the only way I could protect myself, I'm sure that one day I will learn to trust again. I look at life differently, the things that I do, I am unsure that I will ever go back into working with youngsters again, which really hurts a lot as I had so much to offer in the way I was able to have that impact of making someone's life better. With the way that the working environment around youngsters is run now I would feel suffocated, unable to do the work to the degree that it requires. I respect rules, the regulations, but I feel that it's those codes of conduct that are placed on support workers these days is what is leading to a lot of youngsters having mental health issues. The youngsters of today sense that no one has time for them, well, the time that is required, the system is overrun with waiting lists for counselling sessions, other support networks, then when a child is finally allocated a support worker the process is so hit and miss that the child never gets that connection with whoever the worker is, resulting in them never truly opening up. The time between their sessions can also be a deficit to the outcome as it can often be weeks between sessions, by which time the child has either forgotten what was discussed in previous sessions, or they have moved on, and subsequently lost interest in the whole process. This then leads to the child feeling as though they are not really being heard. I have seen and heard it from youngsters that they feel it's a waste of time as they feel that they're not making any progress.

You can't blame the support worker; they are only doing what they have to do with the time that they are allocated which just isn't enough for a lot of these youngsters. It becomes a box ticking task, then as the support worker has ex amount of youngsters that she or he has to get through in a set amount of time, they too are probably frustrated by this as they know themselves it takes time to build up that understanding of a youngster, what makes them tick, and finding out how to impact in the right way to make things better for them. I suppose in a way my role was that unique that I got to spend five days a week with a number of youngsters. Every day I would see each of them, which in turn they very quickly established that there was someone there for them without fail whenever they required reassurance.

I had a vision a few years back about setting up my own foundation that was to be a totally free initiative for 11 to 18-year-olds. After working in schools as well as on projects with kids that don't attend school my idea was to offer free time to youngsters at any level, to set something up that would work alongside the likes of the Youth Sport Trust as well as work in conjunction with the youth zone centres that are starting to pop up around the country. It would have added a huge benefit to the already growing work that is being ploughed in by local authorities. With the added benefit of it being totally free then it is accessible to every single young person out there. It's hard to swallow that I now feel my vision, my dream may never come to fruition after what I have been through that all came about from helping and saving a young person's life. I look at helping people in a different light now, it's dreadful that I have been made to look upon it like that, but it almost rings true that you can't do right for doing wrong, at the end of the day if you can't extend your support to someone that has asked you a question, someone that you have worked alongside of five days a week for almost six months to drag them back to believing in themselves once more, a person that knew you were there should they need a life line. Well, I don't know what the world is coming to. I wouldn't ignore anyone under any circumstances just because I have moved to another working venue, I have strong morals, standards and beliefs, to simply cast them to one side through fear of what others might say when it's in reference to my work, well, my beliefs tend to take the lead, the driving force behind what I do. So when I simply replied to a message from someone I had worked with I didn't realise it would cause such a drama that would unfold against me, drag on for five months, leaving me with mental health issues, depression and having suicidal thoughts. So it was unconventional for me to continue with support, to offer some words of encouragement to someone that obviously looked up to me for reassurance, someone fearing the unknown a little as I was not going to be around on a day-to-day basis as a sounding board once they returned to their studies. Of course, it is going to be a massive transformation even for the most versatile person, but for this one particular individual it was to be a big step, for they had spent the good part of the previous five months just excepting their purpose in life, building their strength up to deal with everyday life. I can fully understand why they would have had some jitters and want to seek the advice from somebody they respected. There had been shit times, there had been excellent times, but the main difference between their life before they worked with me to their life since is that they have the confidence to recognise their challenges, anxieties, and are able to address them as they see fit, but more importantly is that they have a life that is not always dictated by uncertainty and doom.

Some people may view the small achievements of the student that I helped as proof that she simply grew out of her low self-esteem, or that she was actually never affected by it too much in the first place as it may have just been a stage in her natural development. Quite often young people are too scared or feel inwardly that asking for help is a sign of weakness, they may feel that they are embarrassed to do so. For me I was ashamed to talk to anyone about myself, I felt that no one would understand my anxieties, the way that they were affecting me, also the circumstances that led to them being so prominent.

After all this happened I wasted too much time being lost, isolated, asking myself why, my mind running wild, masking the realisation of the situation until that one evening whilst sleeping in the back of my car up on the Trough of Bowland. Busting for a wee at 2 o'clock in the morning I scrabbled around looking for where I had left my trainers, the dim interior light not really being of any assistance to my search, the windows covered in condensation obscuring my view. I opened the door to a lonely silence, the vast shear darkness of being miles from civilisation with no light pollution, I could just about see my feet in front of me. As I stood there, my sleepy eyes still adjusting, I glanced to the sky. There right above my head was the Milky Way. I gazed in a mesmerised state, millions of miles from one side to the other, an infinity of stars and light. I could not stop staring as I stood there in my T-shirt and boxers feeling the cold, but with no urgency to climb back into the car to reacquaint myself with the warm sleeping bag. I must have stood silently for 25 minutes viewing no fewer than four shooting stars in that time frame. All the turmoil of the past few weeks that I had been overwhelmed by disappeared, I was left with a clear focused mind.

At some point in our lives many of us may have the feeling that we feel out of place, we may find it very difficult to find where we fit. No matter what age you are at, or living circumstances, you may be somewhere and stumble upon somebody who inspire us, someone that will encourage you to try something different, to challenge you. Life is about being surrounded by people that care. Far too many people create negative noise, it's a constant battle of refusing to fear failure, never losing hope, using the experience that you have had to fuel your own personal growth, to keep pushing your boundaries, knowing and believing that everything that you are doing is making a difference. Once you understand your why, you will become unstoppable. Gazing into the vast void that was above my head that night gave me the time as well as the space I needed to pick out that one vision, that one inspiring moment to go forward with my life. It was enough to push all of the anger, the insurmountable frustration that I had built up, the anguish I was feeling that was brought about by other people's decisions about the way I had acted as well as the disrespect that they had shown to the bigger picture of what surrounded the situation that they did not take into account when deciding my fate. I came so close to taking my own life, and for what – what other people thought of me. Stars can't shine without darkness, and in the midst of that night I was surrounded by millions that's allowed me to see the greater picture of my life in which the next chapters will flourish with joy at every breath.